WOMAN

Torch of the Future

TORKOM SARAYDARIAN

Woman, Torch of the Future

© 1999 The Creative Trust

First printing 1980 Aquarian Educational Group
Second printing 1999 T.S.G. Publishing Foundation, Inc.

All Rights Reserved

No part of this publication may be reproduced, stored in a retrieval system, or transmitted in any form, by any means, electronic, mechanical, photocopying, recording or otherwise, without permission in writing from the copyright owner or his representatives.

ISBN: 0-929874-33-1
Library of Congress Catalog Card Number: 80-67680

Printed in the United States of America

Cover Design: *A Graphic Design Studio*
                Sedona, AZ

Printed by: *Data Reproductions*
                Rochester Hills, Michigan

Published by: T.S.G. Publishing Foundation, Inc.
                P.O. Box 7068
                Cave Creek, AZ 85327-7068
                United States of America

Note: Meditations, visualizations, and health information are given here as guidelines. They should be used with discretion and after receiving professional medical advice.

Published from donations to the
Torkom Saraydarian Book Publishing Fund

Torkom Saraydarian Book Publishing Fund

Torkom Saraydarian dedicated his entire life to serving others in their spiritual growth. At the time of his passing in 1997, more than 100 manuscripts had been written and remain unpublished. This work represents a seamless tapestry of Wisdom and we are dedicated to publishing the entire collection.

Torkom Saraydarian had the unique wisdom and dedication to write all of these magnificent books in one lifetime. Now it is our turn to do the work. Together we can make his dream a reality and bring his legacy to fruition.

We depend on contributions for the publishing of the books. A special fund, *The Torkom Saraydarian Book Publishing Fund* has been established for the completion of this legacy. Contact us for details about the *Book Fund* and an update regarding remaining manuscripts. You can contribute funds for an entire book, or give any amount you wish on a continuous basis or a one-time contribution.

Thank you for your loving and continuous support.

See back of book for additional information.

Table of Contents

A Few Words vii
Prelude ix
Introduction xv
1. The Foundation 1
2. Marriage 37
3. The Marriage Ceremony 65
4. Choosing the Baby 83
5. The Mother-To-Be 93
6. New Mother Guides 123
7. The Child 137
8. The Father 165
9. The Responsible Woman 183
10. Education and the Child 203
11. Religion and the Child 223
12. Torchbearers 231
    Index 271

A Few Words

This is a book for woman, for the future woman, no matter if she has a child or not.

When I say "woman," I am referring to her heart, to her Intuition, to her natural sense of beauty, compassion, purity, and sacrifice. It is only the heart of a woman equipped with these virtues that will save our culture, our civilization, and build a future for humanity.

People think sacrifice is a painful and humiliating process of giving. This is not what sacrifice is. Sacrifice, for a woman, is to create an atmosphere for the transformation of her beloved ones. Her sacrificial acts are proof that she can be trusted in the darkest moments of our lives. Sacrifice, for a woman, is the moment of ecstasy and joy.

Prelude

When I was
leaving
my home
to walk on my own feet
and trace the thread
of my destiny, my Mother
looked at me
with stern eyes
and said,

> "I feel I will never see you again,
> but you will be always
> in my heart
> if you follow the
> direction of your Soul
> and beware of chaos.

"Direction exists
only
on the path of beauty,
goodness, and truth.
All other paths lead
us into chaos.

    "Chaos is a situation
    in which
    you feel abandoned,
    or you run
    after your tail
    or you crucify
    things
    you worshipped.

        "Chaos is
        a situation
        in which
        you deny your essential
        divinity,
        your dignity.

"Chaos is a situation
in which
your pleasures are your
goals,
and your vanity is your
guide.

"Chaos is a situation
when there is anarchy
within your mind
and your heart."

    I never forgot
    her words.
    Every time
    I fell down,
    the hands, the blessed
    hands of my Mother,
    were
    holding my hands.

When she had finished her
words,
I kissed her hands
and jumped up on the carriage,
and my Father
hurried on
to take me to the
train station . . . .
For three minutes I saw her, in her
white garment and standing
as I left her . . . .
When I couldn't see her
any more,
I said, "Father, stop a minute."
"Why?"
"I want to go back

to the corner of the street
and see if Mother is still there . . . ."

    Father looked
    at me as if he knew my thoughts,
    and in silence
    turned the horses
    back . . . .

We stood at the corner of the street.
Mother was there . . . . She saw us.
Then with her right hand
she made a cross
and blessed me . . .
and went home.

    After a silence of
    half an hour on the road,
    "Father," I said, "she blessed me . . . ."
    "Your Mother
    is a great woman.
    She blessed you, yes, she did.
    And her blessing
    will always
    be with you . . . ."

Mother,
I know
how much
you suffered
for me.

The Prelude xiii

This book
is to tell you
how much
I loved you
and admired your
beauty.

Introduction

In my youth I visited many esoteric centers, brotherhoods, and communities. I met some Sages and Initiates who were intensely interested in the welfare of humanity.

In the course of my relations with esoteric centers and communities and their leaders and guides, I noticed that they were putting a great emphasis on the fatherhood of the man and the motherhood of the woman and virtually were preparing the youth to hold the responsibility of parenthood.

I met many people and communities who were thinking to create a new generation that would, in the future, lead humanity and bring in a new society. They were feeling that the way humanity was presently dealing with family life and its responsibilities was not satisfactory, and they were pointing out the defects in the family relationships that should be corrected if we expect to have a better human life.

They were not satisfied with the marriage laws and rules of the nations. They were seeing the degeneration of true morals and a lack of responsibility in the leadership of religious, political, scientific, and educational organizations. And they were trying to present an alternative to humanity. Family for them was a sacred unity, the foundation stone of the nation and humanity.

They were seeing that the increase in pornographic literature and movies was speeding up the degeneration of the family as well as that of the human race, and they also were aware that the educational institutions were showing a great irresponsibility toward the sacredness of the family unity.

They used to talk about the possibility of a new spirit that could penetrate into the hearts of the youth and inspire them to start a new revival of the family life.

What I intend to share here is a fraction of what I heard and observed.

Chapter One

The Foundation

In one of the monasteries there was a course of study called "five-pointed responsibility." This course was given only by invitation and under strict secrecy in order to prevent many attacks, in many forms, by contemporary authorities. The course lasted five years for males, with a similar course given for the girls.

1) The first year's topic was the anatomy of sex and how it related to the body, emotions, mind, and society.
2) The second year's topic was marriage and its main responsibilities.
3) The third year's topic was the woman: her physical, emotional, mental, spiritual, and social existence as a wife and mother.

4) The fourth year's topic was the man: his physical, emotional, mental, and spiritual responsibilities as a husband and a father.
5) The fifth year's topic was the child — how to raise the child and what responsibilities one has in bringing a child into the world.

The students were taken into the classes when they were 14 or 15 years of age so that they would be ready for marriage, if they so chose, at 21.

The Teachers thought that without the strong foundation of such a course of teaching, the family could not survive, or if it survived, the social problems would increase and add to the misery of humanity. After graduating from such a course, one had a totally new approach toward sex and marriage and family life.

As a result of such courses, the inhabitants of the communities tried to put the teaching into practice. The parents were given the duty to perform investigations of those young women or young men whom their children wanted to marry. The young people could choose their partners quite well after taking the five-pointed responsibility course, but it was the duty of the parents to make a thorough investigation and approve their child's choice.

The family of the boy or girl organized a research or investigative group that was made up mostly of elderly women, in the case of the girl; or elderly men, in the case of the boy. They would have to create ways and means to meet the chosen girl or boy. For example, in the case of the girl the most common way was to invite her to the Turkish bath and there observe the different parts of her body. If the girl took the "test," the elderly ladies met and talked about the different parts of her body and would come to an agreement to reject the girl then and there or to continue further investigation. They used to say that human beings pay more attention when they are buying a horse than when they are marrying a man or a woman! The parents wanted their son or daughter to have beautiful children with beautiful bodies in order to perpetuate the nobility of the family.

I remember one of the investigators discussing a bunch of hair they saw between the breasts of a girl. It was a serious point of discussion as to whether the girl was qualified or not. "That is not a good sign," said one of the investigators, "for it shows an uneven distribution of certain hormones . . . ." I did not understand the remark as I was only ten or eleven years old and a very innocent boy who was following the elderly women with extreme curiosity.

In olden days a wrong marriage could be a cause of catastrophe and even a cause of a fight or a war. The people were forced to be very discriminative from the point of view of heritage, morality, and the reputation of the family. They used to say that a tall building can only stand upon a firm and healthy foundation, and therefore they used to think that a harmoniously built body, a beautiful body, was the outer expression of the inner being of the person.

On one occasion the women were discussing the legs of the girl under investigation. They said she had short legs and it was a sign of this or that, or she had long legs and that was the sign of such and such . . . . They discussed her eyes and said, "Her eyes are too close to each other, too small." No one knows how accurate they were in their judgment and discussion, but one thing was evident: the couples they had investigated before marriage and had passed had the most handsome and beautiful children, and divorce was practically non-existent.

If we count the money we spend, the pain and the anxiety we pass through in a divorce in contemporary society, then we have serious reason to note the marriage customs, rules, and laws of such people who created happy homes, healthy and beautiful children, and a very high standard of morality and honesty.

The investigative group was sworn to secrecy. It was the most serious crime to speak out about the results of their investigation, except to the parents of the young man or woman. When the girl or boy did not meet the requirements, they had the most gentle, courteous, and polite ways to reject them. Most of the investigations were even carried on without the knowledge of the girl or boy or their parents in order not to hurt them in case there was a reason to reject them.

After the first investigation, and the physical body was approved by the investigators, they had very sneaky ways in which the boy or girl was able to see the naked body of the other in order to give final approval. In such cases, for example, a few girl friends of the girl in question came under the instruction of the investigative committee. They were instructed to take the girl to a little lake or river where they would swim naked while the boy was hidden under a bush or behind a rock to see the body of the girl. They did the same for the girl, in order for her to see the body of the boy. This was a most exciting step on the path of investigation, and the girls or boys in charge were secretly rewarded for their inventiveness and discretion.

The second investigation was carried on along the line of the health of the girl or boy and her or his family. They used to go as far back as one hundred years into the history of the family to find out if there were cases of

1. degenerative diseases
2. cancer
3. syphilis
4. gonorrhea
5. tumors
6. heart disease

7. brain diseases
8. epilepsy, diabetes, etc.

The research team used to find out how the ancestors of the girl or boy passed away, from what diseases. They used to see if the parents were healthy and if the sisters and brothers were healthy. They believed that some diseases not only extend four generations but even seven generations, and in various cycles the disease hits the offspring of the family.

One may argue that such an investigation creates a great hindrance for marriage, but one can also say, why perpetuate the sickness, diseases, pain, and suffering in the coming generations? Today we have a great problem in the population explosion. Cannot such a slow and discriminative choice be one of the main answers to this problem?

The second step on the line of the health investigation was the search for any sign of mental disease in the family tree. They wanted to find out if any family member of the girl or boy was hospitalized in a mental hospital or was under care in an asylum. They firmly believed that mental disorders were highly hereditary and cyclically could hit the members of the coming generations. They used to find out if there was any case of mongolism, insanity, and so on.

Suicide was another important point. It was a very serious case if the candidates had any member in their family tree who had killed himself or herself. Suicide was considered an act against the Life Giver and a very black mark on the records of the family.

Divorce was another serious point. The research team had to find out if there were any divorce cases in the family and the reasons for them. If the divorce was the result of a bad choice and children had not been born from it but the candidate was born out of the second marriage, then the case was lighter and more favorable to him or her.

It was thought that divorce was a very important point that could disclose many hidden causes in the family that were not favorable to a healthy home. If the choice for marriage was made consciously and with a thorough investigation, the chances of divorce would be almost nil.

The record of crimes was another point of investigation. The family should not have any criminal records in order for the candidate to be highly qualified for marriage. I remember one girl who was refused because her brother had killed a girl in his anger. The whole village knew about this and the family was not able to erase that black mark from its records, no matter how much the family tried to help others, financially, morally, and in other ways.

Of course, these were extreme measures to take, but they wanted an ideal marriage. We can have some difficulty in understanding these measures at this time in our contemporary history, but the main intention was not to marry for personal interests or pleasures but to create superior offspring who would teach humanity the ways of greater health, greater beauty, and a greater future.

Most of the children coming into the world are unwanted or are children for whom no preparation has been made in order for them to have the best conditions in which to live. If the present situation continues to be the way it is now, our future children will be born in a more polluted atmosphere and in conditions not favorable to their health and growth.

At present, we have more freedom and more sophisticated methods to find out whatever we need to know about our future wife or husband, if passion and other minor interests do not hypnotize and block our vision. For example, many men at this time marry a woman for her legs, and her legs are the answer to all they want to know about the woman.

If we think seriously, we will see how much pain and suffering we are causing our children because of the lack of right choice and right marriage. We are responsible for our children's suffering, pains, and failures. In what way can we justify ourselves if we did not take all precautionary steps but brought children into the world to satisfy our instincts, our parents, or as the inevitable fruits of our pleasures?

Chapter One

After the complete physical nature of the candidate was thoroughly investigated, the next step in the case of the girl was to find out about her heart qualities. Was she kind, generous, patient, loving? Did she have respect toward the elderly, toward her parents, or was she cruel, indifferent, cold and willful, or stubborn? They used to say that the heart quality of the woman is the magnet of the family. It is the heart that cures, transforms, builds, and creates. It is the heart that evokes the best in the husband and the children.

The investigators would deepen their research and find out if the girl loved children, Nature — the trees, flowers, animals, birds. Once I remember an investigative group having a girl baby-sit a small baby so they could see how she would do, but the baby cried so much that the girl, in anger, hit the child and then walked out of the house. Of course, she was taken off the candidate list immediately because the investigators said she could not possibly be a good mother. It is very difficult, they said, to train the heart, as most of the virtues of the heart are inherited or cultivated for generations.

One of the important points of the investigation was the respect shown to elderly people. They tested the girl and boy again and again to find out if he or she loved, respected, and was eager to serve them in their time of need. In those days, they did not have rest homes, homes for senior citizens, or hospitals. The youth were dedicated to caring for their parents when they were in their declining years. No family wanted to have a bride or groom who was not raised to love elderly people and to please them to a certain degree. They also thought that some affectionate attitude with elderly people was a sign of maturity, solemnity, and wisdom.

In several countries, many of the youth liked to gather around elderly people and hear about their experiences in many fields. They liked to find out their viewpoints about important religious, economic, and political questions. Some of the elderly people were retired artists, writers, or people of high position; the youth considered it a privilege to be with such people and collect wisdom from them so that they could conduct their lives better.

Another point for investigation in the case of the girl was to find out her tendency toward education, arts, crafts, music, philosophy, sciences, or if she knew sewing, knitting, or needlework. In the community the young girls were the busiest ones, always doing something. They had their own free times at festivals, family gatherings, sports, but besides all these, they were put in responsible positions on the farms: cooking, cleaning, watching over their younger brothers and sisters, and occupying themselves with needlework, knitting, sewing, arts and crafts, or engaged in some serious study. It was said that a lazy girl is the agent of Satan.

The investigators were also interested if the bride-to-be knew how to cook in such a way that right nourishment was given to the children and family. Most of the families had special recipes that were given to them by their experienced ancestors, for they knew which food had the best minerals and vitamins and what to cook for the special needs of the person. If the family needed more iron, they had different vegetables for it. If they needed potassium or magnesium, then different things were cooked. In short, their food was very balanced because you could see healthy and joyful people with energy and enthusiasm around you. They used to make a wonderful soup with the right combinations which contained full nutritional value. There were a few families who had classes in cooking and arranging the kitchen in such a way that it could serve best for all aspects of cooking.

Another object of investigation was to find out if the bride-to-be was tidy, clean, organized, and economical. The investigative team used to create opportunities to visit the girl's home and check the kitchen, bathroom, and bedroom to see if she was tidy and clean, for it was usually the duty of the young girls to keep the house in good order. They would visit her at different times of the day to see how she was dressed and what was the condition of the home. Once I heard a lady telling one of the other investigative team members that even though the girl in question was tidy and clean, the lady had been shocked at the state of the garden, for the roses and other flowers had not been watered and the weeds were growing wild. She was wondering why this was so. The other team member answered her by saying that the girl's father had been sick and that was probably the reason the girl had not had the time nor the inclination to take care of the garden. This answer did not alleviate the questioning member's doubt . . . .

The girl should also be economical. One of the important virtues of a woman was economy. If she was wasteful, greedy, and hungry for everything she saw, that was the end of the investigation. They wanted the girl to have the spirit of contentment and not use any kind of force on her parents to collect more jewelry or furniture or to replace it without reason, or to buy things that were not essential and thus waste money. They used to say that wastefulness was a sign of lack of discrimination and planning, and a good wife must have discrimination, contentment, and planning.

Some elderly people used to explain to the young girls what economy does for a family, how they could use old dresses by making carpets, bed covers, or different dresses for the children. They told them how the food could be economized, how the house could be taken care of in such a way that the water, the gas, and other materials were not wasted.

I was with a man whose wife said to him as we were leaving his home, "The sleeves on your work jacket are worn out. We can get you a new jacket or I can sew some leather patches on the sleeves, which can extend its life another year." And turning to me she said, "Why to waste money and material?"

I could imagine what an economic catastrophe we would have if suddenly our youth became economical! But I wonder if life will not eventually force such an action upon us.

An organized girl was highly respected. Parents used to plan for picnics, festivals, birthdays, and anniversaries and hand the jobs to the young girls to see how they would manage them. They used to think that a girl who knew how to organize would be able to manage the family in the best way, saving time, energy, and money. To be economical means to spend your money at the right time, for the right object, in the right quantity.

I remember some ladies watching a young girl washing dishes while keeping her busy talking, yet the girl continued to wash and talk with them without wasting a drop of water. Later one of the ladies remarked, "If she knows how to save water, she will also save her husband from lots of worry." Thus one who was economical, clean, organized, and together had a great chance to become a candidate for a good marriage.

The elderly people used to think that our life is a great reflection of what we are inside and that things should be changed inside if we want to change things outside.

The next major investigation was about the sex life of the girl or boy. They tried to find out if she or he were normal; if she had interests in other girls or women or if he had interests in other boys or men; if either of them had had or were having any affairs, or in the case of the girl, if she were pregnant or had had an abortion.

Thus, they tried to find out if the boy or girl had control over their passions and were able to shift their minds to higher occupations whenever excitement knocked upon their doors.

Abortion was considered a crime. There was only one exception, and that was when the mother's life was in danger.

The human soul from the moment of conception is attached to the embryo through the life-thread and slowly penetrates into the body as the embryo grows. At the fourth month, the human soul finally anchors and focuses itself in the pineal body of the embryo. This is why abortion is a crime against the human soul.

We are told that when the embryo is destroyed and its life-thread cut by abortion, the incarnating human soul either tries to obsess the mother and create psychological disturbances in her or wanders in the etheric plane for many years unable to proceed on the path of his evolution. Such souls, when incarnated again, have a deep-seated phobia of death that runs like a thread throughout their life.

If a girl was pregnant from an unmarried relationship, the elderly women knew how to handle the situation quietly. They usually would take the girl to a remote place in the country where she would have the baby in peace and quiet, and then the baby was quietly placed in a home where a couple were not able to have children and were eager for a child. Thus, the girl was freed of the baby.

In these communities, usually no one would marry a girl who was not a virgin.

In this modern world a married or single woman can find many excuses for having an abortion, such as the financial situation, or they have too many children already, or a child will interfere with their careers, and so on. But why must the child be the victim? Why are all these points and excuses not considered and taken care of before conception? A child must not suffer death because of the carelessness of his or her mother. There will always be some couple or some individual who will welcome the child into their home.

Can you imagine if a child has the possibility to take the mother to court for killing him!

Unmarried pregnant girls need our help, as much as we and society can give them. Actually, our society must have professionally organized homes, great structures where the girls can come and find refuge and do their studies or creative works. They can also listen to beautiful music, have discussions, a peaceful time in Nature, and also strictly professional help, medical and psychological help. In such homes, every girl must be free to choose her own spiritual path, without intervention, and to keep or relinquish her religious beliefs.

In these homes they can learn how to raise their children to make them good citizens, and they can learn about marriage and the value of the family. It is also possible to train them in various crafts or professional works so that in the future they can support themselves and even make a good contribution to the home that received them with such great hospitality. The main thing that must be prevalent in such a home is loving understanding and wisdom so as not to cause irritation in the pregnant girls but to help them to give birth to beautiful souls.

They must have their peaceful time and meditation time to create a good psychological atmosphere for their incoming babies and, also, they can have some kind of training to support themselves after the baby is born. This can be extended to include a child-care department, where the children are watched and loved while their mothers are engaged in their work. Let us not forget that in giving our help to a pregnant woman we are decreasing our social and economic problems for the future.

The last and most delicate moment of the investigation was to inform the girl or boy about the investigative team's intention and to reveal the identity of the individual for whom the investigation had been carried out. A few weeks later, when everything was approved by both parties, the girl and boy were taken to a physician for a final medical examination.

If, for example, the girl had not passed the investigation, or rejected marriage with the boy, the whole matter was kept in highest secrecy.

There was another group besides the investigators whose duty was to check the presented information, sort out the information that was not important, and discuss or solve those parts that could be corrected. For example, the researcher might find out that the boy or girl smoked or was hospitalized or had some habit that must be considered. The second group, which was the adjusting and advising group, would take that case of smoking, for example, and find out that the boy or girl had just tried it a few times and dropped it, or could drop it at any time. In this case the elders would speak with the individual and explain to him or her about the consequences of smoking and other related subjects.

As for hospitalization, they wanted to find out the reason for it. If the reason was something that would not reflect on the health and happiness of the family, they would give a positive recommendation.

As for the habits, they would check the nature of the habit and then speak with the boy or girl about it to see what changes could be made.

Many of the boys and girls were advised to return to the special school and renew the five-pointed responsibility course. We do the same in the case of issuing drivers licenses. One cannot obtain a license until he passes the test. Let us not forget that many miseries and future complications can be avoided if such a procedure is taken in deep honesty.

I had the privilege of speaking with some great women who were advisers and sources of wisdom for their families and clans. They said that mothers are considered the foundation stone of the spiritual structure of the world, and for that reason the girls were raised for the sacred duty of motherhood.

The mothers in these villages were the instructors for their daughters. The daughters were told that their supreme duty was to be a mother and that they should prepare for it and be graduated to do so. The young girls enthusiastically performed their duties and responsibilities to reach the honor of becoming a wife, a mother, and eventually a grandmother.

The young girls were instructed how to choose the right man, a man of health, beauty, energy, and intelligence. Many, many occasions were created for a young man to reveal himself: his health, his beauty of character, his energy, and his intelligence.

On these occasions great games were organized in which the girls and women could see the men in action and were able to discriminate between those who were healthy and those who were weak; between those who had integrity and beauty and those who were sneaky, unrighteous, and opportunists; between those who had creative skill and those who were mechanical and uncreative; between those who knew how to use their intelligence and those who were only muscles and bones.

During the various games, the boys were challenged to demonstrate their best not only in sports but in debates and leadership fields also.

The girls, observing the boys over a long period of time, developed a pretty good discrimination of whom to consider as possible candidates for marriage. If a girl had made up her mind about a certain man, she was given the opportunity to have a closer friendship with him and to observe him in regard to his mind, his qualities, and his maturity.

The first duty of parents and leaders of the communities was to provide the opportunity for the girls to choose their mates and the opportunity for the boys to choose their beloved ones. It was only after long years of observation that a noble girl would make a decision about marriage to a special man.

In all ways the girl's family took the right to investigate the boy to find out if their daughter would be safe in marrying such a man. The group of investigators were to find out if the boy was

1. healthy
2. loving and considerate
3. brave and courageous
4. patient
5. diligent
6. educated
7. skillful and generous
8. honored in society and without criminal records
9. full of various virtues
10. fearless
11. not using cigarettes, alcohol, or any kind of drugs
12. of high morals and honest

There was a family who wanted to find out about the generosity and nobility of a certain boy. They told him they were going on a picnic and invited him along. On the way they stopped at a grocery store to buy a few things they needed. After bringing the food to the counter, one of the men said, "Oh I do not have any money with me." The other said, "I have some, but let me see, it is not enough . . . ." Immediately the bridegroom-to-be interrupted and said, "Leave it to me. Let me pay for all of it. And I think we need a few more tomatoes, a little more bread, a little more fruit . . . ."

They went and got the rest of the food, and he paid for all of it. Later, the elderly people looked at each other and smiled.

During the picnic, one of the elderly people went up to the boy and said, "You know, I found my money in my inner pocket. Here, let me pay you back for all the food."

"No," said the boy, "I would rather not take it for, if you will not feel hurt, I consider it a great pleasure to be able to spend such a small amount for my respected friends."

The man did not say anything to him but kissed him on his forehead, which was a sign of great honor.

The courage of a boy was tested in dangerous situations, in times of flood, fire, earthquakes, in hazardous conditions, or in fights.

Education and a profession were very important points. A boy must have skill and be able to support his family without depending upon his parents or relatives. He should have a business or an occupation in which he works with honesty and earnestness. He must be creative, and in any case of emergency, he should be able to adapt himself to various jobs or labors to support his family in at least a moderate way.

Thus, the parents used to prepare their son for an independent life, training him in an occupation and, if the boy proved himself, giving him land, a farm, or other trades which the boy could develop and make into a successful career during his life.

Those boys who were not able to have a serious occupation or were not respected in the business circles were not considered to be men but children who needed to grow.

The boy should also be courageous and fearless. A candidate, who had been highly considered, failed to marry a very precious girl when it was found out that he was a coward.

It was an afternoon when some young people were dancing and having a good time with their families, and the boy had been invited. After a while, as they were all resting, a huge man took a revolver and shot three or four times in the direction of the boy. The boy became pale and began to tremble and was not able to stand up. For half an hour he was very confused. He was rejected as a bridegroom-to-be "because," said an elderly man, "he has no courage, he is not manly, and he cannot defend his family."

I often wondered if the old man was right in his judgment. Does one really need to be fearless to marry a woman and raise children in a world where only the brave can survive? Is cowardliness a sign of spiritual deficiency, lack of psychic power, glandular malfunction, or the result of hidden impressions within the psyche? Does a woman want to marry a brave man? Is it an instinct in her?

Three elderly men took a candidate to a river where a test had been arranged for him. Someone upstream threw a lamb into the water, and as the lamb was being carried down the river, one of the elderly men screamed, "Hey! A lamb! A lamb is drowning!"

Upon hearing these words and seeing the plight of the lamb, the boy immediately took his boots off and jumped into the river and brought the lamb back. It turned out to be only a straw-filled lambskin; when the lambskin was brought to the shore, one of the elderly men said, "You are a man, and that should mean a lot to you."

The reputation of both families of the future couple was a very interesting factor. Our present day youth are not interested in the reputation of the family as their only interest seems to be if the partner is able to satisfy his or her few requirements. Once a family prevented its daughter from marrying a boy whose father was running a gambling business, while the girl's father was a surgeon. This broke the hearts of the young people who sincerely loved each other.

I presented this case to my Father and said, "If two people really love one another, why must they consider the social levels and reputations of the families?"

"Such a rule seems very easy to reject," said my Father, "but remember, that rule is based on the experience of many thousands of years. There is karma involved, subjective influences are involved, and in many cases such unions end with disaster."

"What does an innocent girl or boy have to do with the reputation of the father, if she or he has nothing to do with the reputation?"

"This is not a matter of pity; this is a matter of choosing the best in all aspects. The purpose of true marriage is to achieve an ideal family life, which eventually, if multiplied, will prevent degeneration of our modern social life and prepare homes for future disciples, initiates, or great heroes. If you want further explanations, I would say that the children will be held responsible for the moral debts of the parents."

"But," I said, "is there any hope for an innocent child who is born into a family with a bad reputation?"

"Of course. He or she must be educated and 'washed out' until he is ready to prove that he broke the karmic debts of his family, and he must prove it by the way he lives. Then chances will be given to him to associate with those who have higher standards."

"People think that a reputable family is a rich family. Is this true?"

"No, it is not. Some rich families are very degenerated, and with their power they can impose their will on others and even cover their manifold crimes. There are many great souls in not-so-rich families. Reputation is based on honesty, trust, faithfulness, and on heart qualities. Even mental qualifications do not make a man honest, trustworthy, or faithful.

"Reputation is the fragrance of spiritual achievements. Sometimes social positions and lots of money act as traps to hinder the spiritual evolution of man, and sometimes an honest effort to support a family with a modest income provides conditions for better spiritual progress."

This conversation with my Father took away some pressure that had been accumulating in me from occasionally overhearing various reports of different boys and girls and the rejections and judgments.

How can we handle the reputation problem in this age? Shall we forget it? Or consider it? How far must it go? Do our accumulating files of divorce problems shed a light on these questions? Is the increasing crime all over the world related to families with low reputations?

The future investigators will tell us the facts.

I never have forgotten the day I was with my Teacher when he was talking about a man who tried to operate a whorehouse in a neighborhood village. He said to me, "His father had a bad reputation; many crimes were committed by him in those villages. Often the children are the continuation of their families if they are not given the right education and discipline at an early age."

These thoughts were heavy on my heart to such a degree that I was so careful not to bring any blame on my family by doing something against my own conscience and judgment.

I noticed in my conversation with many couples that the most important thing was to have a considerable degree of intuitive perception and understanding if the marriage was going to be successful. Intuitive perception has nothing to do with our profession or social levels. It is a heart quality, and if people have it to some degree, they understand each other, even in trying circumstances. This intuitive perception was looked for by the investigators in private and close moments with the girl or boy. They presented the candidate with various family problems and watched their reactions to them.

I remember a boy who had just married. His father gave him a considerable amount of money, and the boy opened a business. The business was improving week after week, and the boy and his wife seemed happy.

A few months later the new bride's brothers and sisters visited the family and stayed for a few weeks, eating, drinking, and enjoying themselves, creating extra expenses for which the husband was not yet ready. Then at Christmas time the wife wanted him to buy expensive gifts for her four sisters and three brothers. The husband did it, but with regret. Then he saw that his wife was giving lots of groceries and clothes to her family to help them. A year later the tension grew to such a degree between the wife and husband that the husband finally asked her to stop spending so much money on her family. The wife replied, "They are my family and I must help them."

"But I am not yet in any condition to spend so much money because of my new business," said the husband.

"You don't love us," she cried.

"I love you, but all these added expenses are making my new business fail!"

"If you object to helping my family, then I am going to leave you." And she left their home and went to her parent's home. The whole village was talking and trying to find a solution . . . and I remember an old man sitting under a tree who told me the following words: "Our ancestors have many words of wisdom. For example, they say, 'A hungry bear cannot dance,' or 'Whoever wants to be friends with a hungry person, let him eat well because later he will have difficulty finding food.' "

I thought these parables were the creation of people who had been hurt, but then I realized that the investigators were anxious to find out the economic situation of both parties, and also to find out if the girl or boy had the tendency to waste. I asked the old man: "Can a girl from a low economic strata live with a man who is rich?"

"Yes, she can," he answered, "if the man can satisfy all that she asks for, but one must remember that generally those people who were deprived of many things develop a certain attitude called 'hungry eyes.' You cannot satisfy such persons once they find the way to milk you for all you can provide them. One must have what they call a 'satiated eye,' an eye that is not hungry and does not want to have everything he sees around him.

"It is also true that a girl from a wealthy family will have a difficult time adjusting herself to a family that is poor. Economic conditions in the family have very potent influences upon the stability of the family."

Is this really true in this day and age? Does the economic condition affect the marriage relationship? Maybe the archives of the counseling offices will be able to answer such questions.

It seems to me that if the couple is advanced spiritually and has the intuitional perception and understanding, they can adjust themselves to financial differences and work out the problems, if hidden psychological pressures do not interfere.

Many times I thought that these old sages were really stuck in their ways, and I spoke about these thoughts to my Father: "Don't you think that we can approach life in new ways?"

"You see," he said, "most people create a complicated and artificial life and then try to adjust themselves to that life. But some people want to live a life based on their own ideals and visions. Life can mechanically drown you if you don't have a foundation. . . ."

It seemed to me that he did not answer my questions, although I now feel that there was a great wisdom in those sages; but how will that wisdom translate itself into terms of modern life? Shall we adjust ourselves to a life without standards or adapt the life to the great standards of honesty, harmony, understanding, freedom? And how to do this . . . ?

Some of our social problems originate from disturbed homes. Many wrong decisions have been given by those in the high positions of a nation because of disturbances in their family life. Many business transactions have failed because of the unpleasant family situations of the executives. It is so important to choose your partner in such a way that you will have the least problems at home because your home life will reflect in many of your outer activities.

Some people try to escape from the responsibilities of family life by living as a single man or woman, but this does not solve the problem if the sex urge is still there and forces them to have relations with different people.

A steady, unmarried relationship with a girlfriend or boyfriend presents many problems. There is the possibility of pregnancy and the refusal by the boy or by the girl herself to marry. Then there is the possibility of abortion or tense, emotional conditions between the boy and girl. Many girls choose to have the baby even if they lose their boyfriends who do not feel any responsibility for the child.

A child without a father will have a difficult time as he is growing up if the mother is under constant pressure from lack of money and other things. A mother with a child and without a husband will face many temptations and problems.

Many friends enjoy each other but do not feel responsible for each other. It is only the sense of responsibility that makes one grow in his heart and in his mind.

There is another effort to avoid such responsibilities in choosing a life of celibacy. But true celibacy is not for the general public. It is an achievement. Unless one conquers his physical, emotional, and mental natures and pays his karmic debts and duties, he cannot enter into a true celibacy in which he dedicates his life for a supreme goal or for a great service.

A celibate life has many difficulties and problems. So does married life. Sometimes married life is a great school for the transformation of the soul, if it is chosen and dealt with rightly. Sometimes true celibacy can perform miracles in one's striving.

Everyone must choose according to his own level and responsibilities. This is why the parents and relatives of the young people in the communities mentioned were very careful in their efforts to help the boys or girls choose the right person as far as possible. They would suggest that they do not marry if conditions were not favorable, or, if one had transcended his family obligations, they challenged him or her to live a life of complete dedication to a great cause.

Once a friend of mine said to me, "If these investigators continue to be so serious about their investigations, I am afraid not too many people will be able to marry."

I did not answer him, but I thought . . . is our goal marriage at all costs? Are we all created to increase the population and satisfy our sexual urges and drives? Or is marriage a friendship? Is there a way that man can be highly normal without a sexual relationship? Is sex really *a must*, or is it used to manipulate people, to create business and exploitation?

I still don't have clear answers to these questions . . . .

I remember my friend looking me in the eye and saying, "Come on now, say something."

"What do you want me to say?" I asked. "You are right, but there is something fundamentally wrong with your thought, and I am not yet clear exactly what it is . . . ."

It seems to me that in certain conditions it is a crime to marry and have children. Those who are not able to meet the responsibilities of family life should not marry and have children. To marry and have children must be for those who are specially schooled and prepared for it, as a man is schooled and prepared to be a doctor or lawyer.

In a few hundred years people will marry and have children only if they pass through certain tests and requirements dealing with their physical, emotional, mental, and spiritual natures, and only then with the permission of higher authorities who, at that time, will be great spiritual physicians or priests who will also be the representatives of the law. Once I asked my Mother, "What happens to the girls or boys who don't pass the investigation?" She answered, "Some of them do marry if the parents are satisfied with a few fundamental requirements. Some dedicate themselves to God and enter convents and monasteries and work in the field of religion. Others go and serve in hospitals, dedicating their lives to the sick. Still others work hard and finish their schooling and work in highly specialized fields. Some of them marry, rejecting the considerations of the moral laws of the community; some of them travel and marry in another country . . . but no matter where they go, they realize that marriage is sacred and to bring children to earth requires a great sense of responsibility." She added, "Only a minority will follow consciously the law of marriage, demonstrating a high level integrity, beauty, health, and leadership quality and they can change the face of the world if they will . . . ."

Higher requirements were a great challenge for both parties. Young people really tried to strive to be an example of beauty, wisdom, and talent and to demonstrate higher virtues.

The cornerstone of an advancing nation is the family unit. Let us build our new civilization upon a highly prepared foundation stone.

There was a girl and boy who loved each other, and the boy wanted to marry her. But the girl wanted him to learn to play the violin before she would decide to marry him. All else was in order, so the boy went for five years to a very great teacher to learn the violin. Then the time came that he gave a great recital for the community, and a few days later the girl accepted and married him. It seems very romantic, but doesn't challenge evoke striving, and doesn't striving makes us to be more than we are? Isn't beingness more important than our pleasures, which may fade away as the years pass? Do not our relations have the subjective purpose to evoke greatness from each other and help each other to go ahead on the path of spiritual perfection? Of course, such a Teaching will not hold any attraction for a materialist who eats and drinks and assumes that life is for pleasure and at the grave everything ends and that is all.

In reading Shakespeare I found the following sonnet, which reflects the psychology of many at present:

> "My love is as a fever, longing still
> For that which longer nurseth the disease,
> Feeding on that which doth preserve the ill,
> Th' uncertain sickly appetite to please.

> My reason, the physician to my love,
> Angry that his prescriptions are not kept,
> Hath left me, and I desperate now approve
> Desire is death, which physic did except.
> Past cure I am, now reason is past care,
> And frantic-mad with evermore unrest;
> My thoughts and my discourse as madmen's are,
> At random from the truth vainly express'd;
> For I have sworn thee fair and thought thee bright,
> Who art as black as hell, as dark as night."[1]

In olden Greece, great philosophers or political leaders used higher rules to produce healthy, beautiful bodies and talented persons. People of these remote communities had one thing in their mind: to improve the life. They thought life was a special school in which you must try your best to reach spiritual maturity and express that maturity in your daily family and social relationships. Their dream was to create a superior man and woman. Were they able to do it? I would say yes. They held the standard high, and here, there, a few daring ones followed their codes of life and achieved great

---

[1.] Charles Sisson, ed., *Shakespeare's Complete Works*, "Sonnet 147," (New York: Harper & Bros., 1953), p. 1317.

beauty and mastery over themselves. Great heroes of ancient and modern times are the fruits of such striving for a vision.

The cornerstone of an advancing nation is the family unit. Let us build our new civilization upon a highly prepared foundation stone.

Chapter Two

Marriage

There was a custom that before the actual marriage the young couple should be engaged for at least 3 to 4 months in order to make the needed preparations for marriage and get to know each other better. If any disagreement should happen, they should try to solve it in the best way possible or else dissolve the engagement. Many future problems were avoided in that way, but many new problems were also created.

We had a family friend, a young girl who had lost her father and mother in her childhood and was living with her foster parents. The foster parents were honest people; they were gardeners and not wealthy.

The girl was an exceptional beauty and had great charm. But after becoming engaged, she would break the engagement. This happened a few times, each time with a different boy.

She was teaching in an elementary school, and one day she came to my Mother for counseling. The counseling was done in my room because I was sick and my Mother did not want to leave me alone.

My Mother respected the girl highly, and she spoke with her in a very loving way, emphasizing the words to make her understand: "I would say that you should not use your beauty and charm to hurt boys. Boys can be hurt deeply if you flirt with them as if you love them, when you really don't mean it. It is a very dangerous game that may bring you some karmic suffering, even if they do not verbally attack you.

"If you give verbal promises to a boy and thus he becomes really attached to you but then for some reason you are not interested in him any longer, then you must be honest with him and state the real reason why you no longer want to make your relation closer. Never hide in lies.

"Do not make the boy feel that he was wrong, or that he was great and it was your own personal problems that must cause you to separate. State your true reasons and be firm; do not be changeable. If you do not know your reasons, examine yourself and find out. Before any engagement, think seriously, or else you will hurt your reputation and no one will dare propose marriage to you.

"The worst thing is to idealize your decision. You should not say that you want to remain single because you want to save your time and energy or you want to study when you have different reasons in mind.

"You were engaged three times, and each time you had mysterious reasons for breaking it off. I do not know why you were not able to decide before becoming engaged, for much information was available to you.

"As I said, it is a dangerous game you are playing, and sooner or later you will ruin your reputation with it.

"When people love each other, they give their hearts to each other to be safeguarded. And the heart is the most precious treasure. One must be very careful to treasure a heart . . . . Do not love easily. Give time to yourself. Do not accept a heart given to you without a deep sense of responsibility. A heart is not an object that you can take and throw in a corner.

"Be careful not to encourage a young man to give his heart to you, for a heart turns into a wild horse if deceived or rejected and not handled carefully. Some girls enjoy flirting, but boys take it seriously and use their imagination to translate the flirting of the girls into feeling, touching, marriage, children, pleasures, etc.

"Once you start such an activity in their mind through your careless manners, dressing, or words, they develop certain emotions in their heart, and these emotions crave satisfaction. If these emotions are not satisfied, sometimes the boys turn to violence or crimes, or lead themselves into inertia, depression, or artificial ways of exhaustion.

"Of course, the same is true of girls if the boys do not watch their relationship with them.

"A girl must not stay aloof but must use one of her secret mechanisms, which is called the 'distance measuring device.' With this device, she can always find out if she is too close to a boy without any reason for it, or if the boy is getting too close to her without conscious invitation.

"The beauty of a woman is her conscious control over the emotions of the man."

Later, my Mother found out that this girl had a great fear of sex. She advised her to go to an old lady who was a great "psychoanalyst" but had never graduated from any college.

Unfortunately, I didn't have the chance to find out how they solved the problem. Neither was I able to get my Mother to reveal any secrets to me. Whenever I asked about the girl she would say, "You mind only your business."

Eventually the girl married, and she had a very happy family.

When the parents of the girl and boy finished their investigation and both had passed, the boy and girl became engaged and the marriage preparations would start.

Before the marriage ceremony, the boy and girl would review the course on marriage and its main responsibilities. In this course, the Teacher would emphasize the ideal attitude of a woman and man toward sex and pregnancy. They were told that marriage does not mean intercourse and sex but a very sacred friendship to bring in advanced souls and provide for them the best physical, emotional, and mental equipment and then to raise these souls in such a way that physically, emotionally, and mentally they would be healthy.

In the marriage the family unit must grow, unfold, and advance spiritually. A family provides the best conditions to learn life's lessons, if it runs on the right track. The Teacher would also explain that earthly marriage is the symbol of the unity of the Inner Guides. Inner Guides are called the Guardian Angels of the couple. These Inner Guides pass through a heavenly marriage when the souls They are guiding have a right marriage. That is why care must be taken not to tolerate any kind of intruder to cause separation between the couple.

Another item that was emphasized was daily worship and a planned procedure of meditation.

Generally, the marriage of today is a contract between two people that gives them an official permit to have sex with one another, to have legal children, and to have legal rights to each other's possessions.

But the *real* marriage goes beyond purely physical concerns. It is a fusion of the man and woman. It is the synchronization or harmonization of the mental plane and the fusion of the two souls into one rhythm.

Real marriage requires intelligent preparation and full readiness for its obligations. At present, the emphasis is on the physical relationship with some emotional and mental cooperation. In the future more and more people will realize that the supreme duty of marriage is to help each other in such a way that the divine Self within each one finds opportunities gradually to manifest Itself. This is the real duty of the married couple — to learn how to live, how to relate with their partner so that the hidden beauty, the hidden divine Self in them begins to manifest Its beauty and glory.

In the future, married couples will go through special training to assist each other to radiate the highest within them. Once I saw a drama in which a man and a woman were trying to climb a huge tree, each acting alternately as a bridge and a climber. This was a great symbol showing that the man and the woman will be the bridge and the traveler alternately. This can be done in a marriage, if the marriage does not revolve around sex, and if the couple tries to create integration, at-one-ment, and eventually a great fusion.

In mystic literature, the Soul is symbolized as the bride with whom the groom is going to be at-one. This is a great symbol teaching us that unless the couple meets each other on the level of the higher mind or the Intuition, true unity is not achieved.

It is very rare to achieve such a conscious unity with one's own Soul. It is also rare to have a conscious union with your partner on the Soul level, but there is no real marriage unless one is also married on the Soul level. This is the "rock foundation" that Christ referred to when He was talking about two men, one of whom built his house on sand and the other on rock. The man who built his house on sand lost it when the psychological and physical flood and wind came and hit the house. But the other house did not move, despite all physical and psychological disasters. Many marriages are built on sand, and they do not endure. Some of the rare ones are built on rock, and they endure forever, despite all tribulations.

To build such a foundation, the couple must have a service project. This is a very important key for great success. Apart from whatever they are able to do individually in any field of service, they must have a goal in which together they unite their hearts and souls — a great humanitarian or global project that evokes greater challenge from each of them, a goal in which they put the blood of their hearts.

The integration and fusion of the couple will be as high as their goal and their dedication to the goal. There is no other way to evoke the highest from each other and meet each other on higher and higher planes of integration.

Later, to accomplish a greater fusion in the family, the children must be challenged to contribute to the common goal. Such a family will be a house built on the "rock of ages."

Concerning sex

In the marriage there must be mutually agreed upon physical discipline concerning

- sex
- various obligations
- various contacts

Sex must not be imposed upon each other, but by mutual agreement the cyclic contact must be decided and appropriate days arranged. Sex should be cyclic.

In the act of intercourse there are many secrets that we cannot learn from our textbooks. Teachers told me that man gives energy and certain secretions to the woman at the time of intercourse. Woman receives these secretions and energy, multiplies them in her organ and in the psychic system, and gives them back to the man as joy and vitality. When the joy and vitality reach the man, the man starts his orgasm, and with his orgasm all his aura and etheric centers are fused with the aura and etheric centers of the woman, forming an electromagnetic funnel for the reception of the thread of life from the one who is ready to incarnate.

Thus, the excitement that man induces into the nature of the woman comes back to him as an energy of love, which has an uplifting and healing effect on him.

In normal sexual intercourse, the positive and negative electricity is combined within the body of the male and female, producing a flame that causes sublimation and transmutation in both parties. This flame nourishes the nervous system, purifies the negative elements gathered within the etheric body, and opens the blocked channels of prana if produced with a lofty spirit, with purpose, and without artificial stimulants.

This is not the case with homosexuality. Homosexuals feed each other with the same female or male energy, which does not create the flame and does not cause sublimation. When the force reaches its maximum voltage, it begins to cause degeneration in their etheric centers and glands, causing, at first, periodic depression and then, gradually, heavy depression.

The creative energy in the natural way of intercourse is like waves penetrating into the emotional, mental, and spiritual bodies and lighting the creative atoms in them.

Such a man and woman feel creative urges and drives and demonstrate creativity in their daily labor, daily duties, as well as in their creative endeavors.

The flame produced in the natural way of intercourse also protects against certain diseases and microbes. But the most important result brought about by natural intercourse is that the male and female reach a completion. For example, in the case of a battery in a car, the positive cable will never make the battery work until the grounding is completed. Such a completion turns into an urge to manifest the completed self. This is how self-actualization starts.

In homosexuality there is mostly the satisfaction of ejaculation. There is no subjective completion, and there is no increasing drive for creativity and self-exertion. It is true that throughout history, homosexuals have left some creative works behind them, but they are of a very mediocre level.

In normal intercourse, the man and the woman enjoy their beingness; they enjoy contrasting themselves to the opposite sex.

In homosexuality, this is only the imaginative and not the real. When a man is going with a man, he is losing his sense of manliness. When a woman is going with another woman, she is losing her sense of womanliness. They are confusing themselves.

In natural sex, the man and woman already have a sense of identity with themselves; there is no need to look for it in the partner. But in homosexuality, there is a perverted effort to come in contact with his or her self through a person of the same sex because their own sense of identity is not there. They look for it in the same sex to make them feel that they exist, for they are not content with themselves. Homosexuality does not ground individuals, and they always feel unidentified. To make a homosexual person natural, you must help him or her to come in contact with his True Self.[1]

It is the opposite sex that gives meaning, measure, and value to our life and that makes us productive or creative.

Intercourse between a man and a woman should not be limited to just the physical act, but the intercourse must proceed into the emotional, mental, and spiritual levels.

In all male and female relationships, all forms of activity are as phases of intercourse, with creative results on various levels.

In some places in Asia, marriage or real love was symbolized by the merging of two flames. The attention was drawn to the fact of fusion of the two flames and to the fact of their becoming one flame.

Intercourse was considered as the beginning of the merging of the two flames. But this flame cannot continue to exist if the emotional, mental, and spiritual fires of the male and female are not continually feeding it.

---

[1] Note: *The Science of Becoming Oneself* is a very helpful book for anyone to make contact with one's True Self.

Every time a man has intercourse, he pays a high price for it, using the jewels prepared by his master gland. One of my Teachers once said that man uses one spoonful of blood to prepare the sperm for one intercourse. If such an expenditure is not rewarded by creating a fusion with the woman, it would be considered a total waste for the man.

In some groups that were dedicated to spiritual adventures, intercourse was considered a sacrifice. On one occasion, I heard a woman talking to her husband as follows: "If you sacrifice, giving me a child . . . ."

In that small community, people married to work for some spiritual project. They used to have one child, or none at all. They were dedicated to service and the creative arts.

I never saw such beautiful people in my life. They were healthy, magnetic, strong, and had a commanding influence. I was told they never had sexual intercourse except when they wanted a child.

Once I asked my Father, "How is it that these people can control their sexual urges and drives?"

"By a technique called the sublimation technique," he answered. "In this technique, they learn to withdraw their consciousness or attention from their sex organs to their head and concentrate it on some great vision, on some great project of service."

"Does their love increase toward each other if they do not relate to each other cyclically?" I asked.

"People think sex is love, and that is true. But if you spend it foolishly, you have less love. See how much you love me, how much you love your Mother and sisters, and how much you love your friends? Some people use only their sex organ to communicate with each other; they do not look for other means of deeper contact.

"It is possible to make love through hearts, through souls, through minds, through the innermost Self. Once we experience such greater loves, we let the sex organs do their predestined work only. But people will realize such facts when they hear the call of a great sacrifice."

In this community, both the families of the girl and the boy were very anxious to build a flame that would become a torch in future generations.

Another time, I asked my Father, "What are the true characteristics of a real man?"

"There are many," he answered, "but the fundamental ones are:

- straightforwardness
- fearlessness
- leadership
- sincerity
- keen intellect
- nobility
- creativity
- magnanimity
- sense of justice

"Woman," he added, "loves a man who has such characteristics. Woman has a keen sensitivity to these virtues. She wants the best. The husband is her pride, her future, her object of worship. Whoever disillusions his wife, loses her trust and love. Nature gave her a higher sense of value so that through her offspring the human race evolves toward higher standards of achievement.

"If woman did not have a keen sense of value, the life would have degenerated a long time ago. That is why we say that when woman loses her sense of value, the nation degenerates."

There was a counseling session for married couples that usually started six months after their marriage. This counseling was arranged in a special way. The couple would sit silently in a room with three elders, one man and two women. The couple would try to answer silently the following questions, which had been given to them at the door:

- How can you increase the joy in your home?
- Do you have any complaints?
- How much do you appreciate your partner?

After half an hour, the elderly gentleman would ask if there was anything the couple would like to discuss. If so, the discussion would start, and the married couple would confront each other if they felt there was a need to do so. Complaints and appreciation, if there were any, were heard from both sides.

If there had been problems discussed, one of the elderly people would then ask the couple if they saw any way to solve the problems they had stated they had. The couple was helped and encouraged to find their own solutions rather than to take advice.

At the end of the session, one of the elders would give the couple some deeper insight into the good of marriage and then, with blessings, the couple would depart.

Such a procedure was cyclic: every six months for three years, then every year for ten years. After that, it was done every three years.

Such help would keep the marriage on a high level and inspire and encourage the young couple to solve their problems and press forward toward greater cooperation and happiness.

My Mother said that the three elders never advised or criticized the couple, but only helped them to see the issues and confront them. Thus, the couple had a chance to review intelligently the way their marriage was going and should be going.

The elders used to encourage the couple to confront each other, but before the confrontation, there was a ceremony that the couple was taught to do. First they would sit in their separate rooms and pray for each other to see the truth and pray that God would help each to obey the truth. Then they would each light a candle and go and exchange the candles with one another. Then they would sit and talk in the light of the candles.

I asked my married sister about this candle ceremony, and she said, "In the light of the candle, people see reality." Then she smiled.

"What does the candle have to do with our understanding?" I asked.

"It is complicated," she replied.

"Please, sister . . . ."

"Well, the candle burns away the unreality wrapped around the truth, such as many selfish motives, emotions, and stupid thoughts, and lets you converse on the basic reality, on facts. . . ."

"How does it do that?" I persisted.

"If you ask more, I will leave you alone!"

I remember jumping on her and hugging her and saying, "Sister, please!"

"Well, you must not tell people who would laugh at you."

"I promise."

"The candle always attracts fiery sparks from space and purifies the atmosphere of the room. Sometimes fiery entities come and illuminate our consciousness, if we are sincere and honest in our motives."

After that conversation, I always used to have a pure wax candle in my room. Whenever I lit the candle, I felt more joyful and more attracted to spiritual values.

Total abstinence from sexual relations at the time of the woman's period was also stressed.

Ancients suggested that the duration of the woman's period be counted as three days before the period, the days of her actual period, and the three days after the end of her period.

Many troubles and complications can be avoided in the family if these rules are observed.

A woman who is having her period must not sleep in the same bed as her husband, and before she sleeps, she must keep her mind occupied with literature that uplifts her. This will help keep her mind focused on higher planes.

Physical contact of any type or form with a woman who was having her period was considered wrong by the ancients. They believed that when a woman is having her period, astral entities or psychic influences of a doubtful nature try to get hold of her. Also, at the time of her period, the woman passes through psychological changes and disturbances, and often it is in these cycles that wrong decisions are made or taken by her. These psychic disturbances increase when any tension is imposed upon her or any heavy demand is put upon her. Because of these reasons, the husband is to leave her be and not create any pressure upon her, make her nervous with his demands, or discuss matters that will make her upset or uncomfortable.

In the olden days, when the woman was having her period, she was given a quiet time and relaxation in Nature with beautiful music and literature.

Solemnity in both partners saves many tensions.

At the time of each of the Full Moons — two days prior to it, the day of it, through two days after it — sex was not allowed. The reasons for this were as follows:

1) These five days were dedicated to spiritual unfoldment, to meditation, to prayer, and to intensive aspiration toward high ideals.
2) During these days, it is possible to come in contact with one's own Transpersonal Self and bring greater creative energies to the world.
3) The Full Moon light may stimulate lower urges and drives and disturb psychic wounds in one's own nature. One needs energy, will power, and striving to avoid such psychic and psychological attacks.
4) At Full Moon times, the Sun releases greater amounts of energy to the planet. This energy must be used for higher creativity, or else it will energize the "weeds" of our nature.
5) Sexual contact during these five days decreases the sensitivity of the etheric and mental bodies to higher impressions coming from conscious sources.
6) It is also a great discipline for the wife and husband to relate to each other on higher planes rather than on sexual levels.
7) Of course, heavy food intake was also avoided during this time.

Oral sex was strictly forbidden for the following reasons:

1. Many germs that will not affect or cause serious problems to the couple when passed from one to the other's sex organs will seriously affect the couple if done by mouth, for the germs can spread to the lungs, ears, and eyes and also to the digestive system. Let us remember that the sex organs are also organs of elimination, and urine and various other secretions can contain numerous germs.

2. Esoterically, the throat center is the higher counterpart of the sex center, and there is a great relation between the glands and the centers. The throat center is far more advanced than the sacral center, and in comparison to the sex center, it has a much higher frequency of vibration. The coarse and crude sphere of the sex center can retard the throat center and interfere with its complicated duties, and thus it may develop many organic troubles. On the other hand, the highly developed throat center can cause a great stimulation in the sacral center and sex organs and cause many diseases in them. It is just like engaging two gears of various speeds or blowing up a balloon beyond its capacity.

The complications gathered in the sex and throat centers affect our emotional and intellectual life and often lead us into depression and inertia.

3. Oral sex overstimulates the organs, and they, in turn, cause more orgasms than the body can handle and more than the body is capable of continuously producing. Long years of such a practice deprive a person of precious energy, which will reflect in one's physical, emotional, and mental activities.

Many men like oral sex because they have lost the sensitivity in their organ. Some fuses have gone wrong in their minds, and to make their brains register the pleasure of sex, they look for excessive sensations through oral sex. This is a clear sign that man is either lacking in potency or very soon will lose it altogether.

4. The natural way of sex provides a way of deepening love and respect and increasing magnetism and energy. Man charges woman with etheric energy, and woman gives him emotional energy.

In oral sex, the solar plexus and the triangle of etheric energy come and accumulate in these centers without finding a way to flow into each other. This eventually brings many serious problems for the couple.

5. Many men and women who used to practice oral sex suddenly withdrew from sex altogether for years. They said they hated sex. Such a withdrawal is the result of the odors and rotten taste that the man and woman practicing oral sex often experience. That puts an end to their sexual interest, which remains as an inhibition in them.

6. If one of the partners does not like oral sex but is forced or cajoled into doing it for the sake of marital harmony, friendship, or other considerations, he or she loses respect for his or her partner; such a feeling eventually turns into indifference or a feeling of hatred toward the partner.

The degeneration of a family and a nation starts with oral sex and other inhuman practices.

Sexual contact with men or women other than the wife or the husband was considered not only an ugly act, but a breakage of the magnetic link between the two partners. A married couple eventually builds a magnetic cord that extends first from one sex center to the other's sex center; then it connects the couple's solar plexus centers; then it raises to their heart centers and eventually to their Chalices.

These magnetic cords break if loyalty is violated. Sometimes it never rebuilds again, and the cords, like broken branches, leak energy or, in some instances, are used by dark forces to stimulate the lower centers and attack the higher centers of the couple.

The link stays unbroken even at the time of death. It is with such a development of fusion that a couple meets each other, life after life, helping each other's evolution and together reaching higher levels of achievement.

During marriage, one must try to exercise a very high loyalty through the physical body, the emotions, and the mind, and never allow an intruder to sever the link. Some countries in Asia expel a man or woman who seduced a husband or a wife and thus caused separation in the family. Christ strongly emphasized that no one must dare to break up a marriage.

There are certain exceptions in which a marriage can be dissolved, such as when the marriage is only a formal tie. It cannot continue under such false premises. Or after the death of a partner, the remaining partner could decide to remarry if the link had not really been built with the previous partner, and if the surviving partner was sure he or she could build a better union. After a divorce, remarriage was often very rough, with many problems and complications. But in some cases one would find his or her best partner.

Concerning various obligations

Mutual understanding of various jobs and obligations in the home helped the growth of the family. For example, while the Mother is breastfeeding the baby, the Father is doing the cooking and the dishes. The work is to be shared. The ancients believed this creates intimacy and expansion between the couple. Maybe the husband is tired but has brought home some work from the office that has to be done. Then, if the wife possibly can, she will help him with his chores or assume them for that period of time. Or when the Mother is very tired from cooking and cleaning and taking care of the children all day, it is the Father's duty to help and relieve her. It is very important that they share and have the experience of each other's tasks in the home, for the work is to be divided between them.

A sense of responsibility develops when each member of the family alternately does certain tasks. For example, daughters and sons must take part in the household work, the cleaning, the gardening, repair work, painting, and so on. But the important thing is that they all must sit down together and prepare the work program without excluding anyone. Each one must feel responsible to bring his or her part into the life of the family and do his or her share with joy, considering it a privilege. Children raised in such a family will have greater success in outer life.

Of course, excuses will be made, but one must have a real reason to excuse himself from a duty and have someone else fulfill it. Ever so often, the family will have a meeting to discuss the efficiency of the labor being done and, if necessary, point out the improvement needed in certain areas.

Concerning various contacts

In an ideal family, certain old contacts must be discontinued and certain new contacts must be established. Good contacts help family integration. If any contact creates doubts, secrecy, suspicion, then it must be avoided or discontinued.

For example, an ideal family must avoid those people who gossip about others or make ugly remarks about family members. I remember my Mother telling a woman who had been trying to gossip with her that she no longer could carry on the friendship with the lady because my Mother was not interested in hearing about the private lives of other people. The woman left in a huff and I said, "Mother, she was really mad . . . ." She answered, "Sometimes it is important to take decisive action to prevent future complications."

In various places in Asia, a man cannot bring any guest to his home who does not have a good reputation or has relations with doubtful people. The most important thing a family wants to know about a visitor is, "What is his motive?" Good families have a good circle of friends with whom they have dinners, parties, discussion nights, and so on. They used to say that the most precious thing was a friend, but it must be a proven friend. There was also another saying, "Tell me who your friend is, and I will tell you who you are."

Marriage and Celibacy

Marriage and celibacy were approached in the following ways:

If one is really advanced, if he is the master of his sexual urges and drives and is dedicated to a great sacrificial service, he can remain celibate to give the whole of his attention and energy to the task ahead.

For those who have not achieved such a mastery, the best thing for them is to marry, raise children, and be a good, responsible father or mother. The ancients said that a family is a sacred unit, the greatest school for a soul, and a great battlefield where one can dissolve his or her past obligations and get rid of karma.

The ancients also believed that those who had lost their wife or husband and had completed their obligations with their children must retreat from the world and think about their soul salvation or penetrate into their destiny of everlasting life. Many such people either dedicated their life to the service of their country or retreated into the monasteries, convents, or mountains to pursue a serious spiritual path.

There were also those who, because of reasons of health or mental retardation, did not want to marry but worked in society in different fields according to their abilities.

Those who could marry and raise children but did not, because of their lack of morals and continual desire to increase their pleasures with changing relationships, were looked upon as dangers to society. Such people were called "turners in any direction according to the blowing wind."

In the olden communities the celibates were the monks, living in monasteries and appearing only in public to deliver a message. In the monasteries, they were involved in the serious work of meditation, writing books, translating, or copying scripts from the texts. Priests living in the communities, because of their continuous contact with society, were allowed to marry.

There were people who used to live together as wife and husband without religious or legal marriage. But if they lived together continuously for five years, they were counted as married couples before the authorities. Also, if they had a baby from such a relationship, they were counted as married, and there was heavy pressure on the man to meet his responsibilities toward the baby and the mother.

Those who neglected their responsibilities usually would run away and hide themselves in big cities or other countries.

The life was hard, but it was accepted as a normal life. There was hardly any divorce; health was magnificent; crime was rare. Artificial stimulants were almost nil and pornography was a deadly sin.

One day, as I was leaving one of these communities, I spoke with one of the great Dervish Teachers and asked his opinion of sex. He spoke for at least an hour, and the summary of his talk is given here:

"Sex is one of the divine gifts to man from God. It must be used as if it were your last penny in your pocket. It is this energy that is used as a fuel in our system for transformation, transmutation, and transfiguration.

"There should be a period of total abstinence if one wants to make a breakthrough into the mysteries of life.

"All our marriage and sex problems can be solved only if humanity realizes the preciousness of the sex energy and uses it for higher goals.

"Most of our sexual excitement is not natural. It is imposed upon us by the thoughts and actions of other people. When artificial stimulants are cut, man naturally does not want to waste his energy.

"This generation will suffer long in the grip of the sex glamor for the sex humanity is displaying at this time is like that of the Atlantean times in which the misuse of sex was at its peak. But in a few generations this grip will loosen, and normal sex will be restored."

Chapter Three

The Marriage Ceremony

The marriage ceremony itself is considered very important. It is in this ceremony that the union is truly consecrated. This ceremony is to be repeated every third year on the anniversary date.

Consecration means that the union is dedicated to the real goals of marriage, which are to assist the Divine Plan. The goals of marriage can be summarized as follows:

1) To achieve physical, emotional, and mental harmony
2) To give birth to souls
3) To prepare for these souls the best bodies and the best environment possible and to assist them to unfold physically, emotionally, mentally, and spiritually

4) To achieve soul-infusion with the partner
5) To fulfill a creative service for humanity
6) To assist each other to cultivate the virtues of gratitude, tolerance, patience, sacrificial service, courage, joy, and solemnity
7) To assist each other to pass through life in a victorious way

After these goals are realized and discussed by the partners, they must dedicate their lives to fulfill these goals. It is this sincere, solemn, and conscious dedication that builds the foundation of a consecrated family.

The marriage ceremony must be a symbolic ritual, impressing the minds of the partners with the seven goals of marriage in such a way that the symbols always remain in their minds as reminders of their sacred obligations.

The goals of marriage will be symbolized by a "journey" from a door to a consecrated place of prayer, meditation, and worship. If the ceremony takes place in an open field, it is easy to symbolize the "door" by two pillars, poles, or rocks, and the consecrated place with a Holy Scripture, cross, or five-pointed star. The distance from the door to the consecrated place is the distance between birth and death during which the couple will live together and try to perform their sacred duties.

It is on this journey that the officiating minister and his assistant will accompany them as the symbols of the couple's souls and personalities, leading them safely to the fulfillment of their duties. The journey will be divided into seven stages.

In the first stage the couple will perform a ceremony that will symbolize their physical, emotional, mental, and spiritual integration. This ceremony will always be performed in all the other stages as a keynote of the marriage to show that this integration is achieved progressively, steadily, and very gradually throughout the journey of the marriage.

A. The first stage is very simple. After the couple enters the door, they walk a few steps together, then separate and turn to each other and smile. Taking hold of each other's hands and with their feet touching, they will hug each other in a way that their hearts are closest to each other. Then the bride will produce a blue thread with which the groom will make a circle around their waists and tie it.

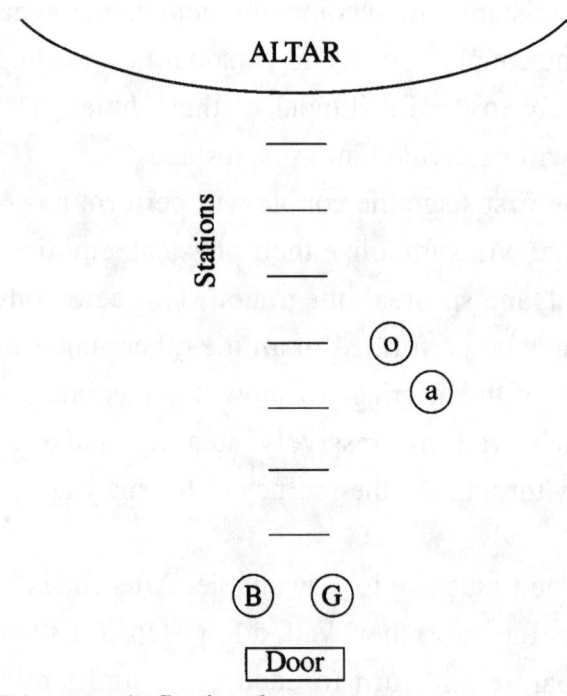

Diagram A, Station 1

These actions will be performed after the following statements or words of power — which the priest or officiant will recite. He will say:

1. *In the name of Beauty, behold the beauty shining within each other's soul.* They smile.
2. *In the name of the One Who is the One in all manifestation, let your hands join and give you the feeling of unity.* They hold hands.

3. *In the name of the Supreme Goal, let your feet contact and walk the way of unfoldment.* They make their feet touch.
4. *In the name of goodness, let your hearts contact and stream forth the love which will feed the garden of your life.* They hug.
5. *In the name of sacrifice, let your life be united so that you walk together, and let no force be capable of breaking the tie.* The blue thread ties them together.

Then the officiant will light the candle of his assistant and order him to lead the couple toward the next stage. The couple will walk, taking united steps, and holding each other at the waist.

B. At the second station or stage, the first four steps of the same ceremony will be performed. Before the fifth statement, a child will bring them two roses. Before giving the roses, the child will place each rose on his (or her) own heart and then give the first one to the bride and the second rose to the groom, Then the child will stand two feet away from them, and the assistant will then extend the circling thread around the couple to include the child. This will be done by the fifth word of power of the officiant, who will say:

In the name of service, let this soul be included in the journey, to unfold like the roses he presented to the travelers on the Path.

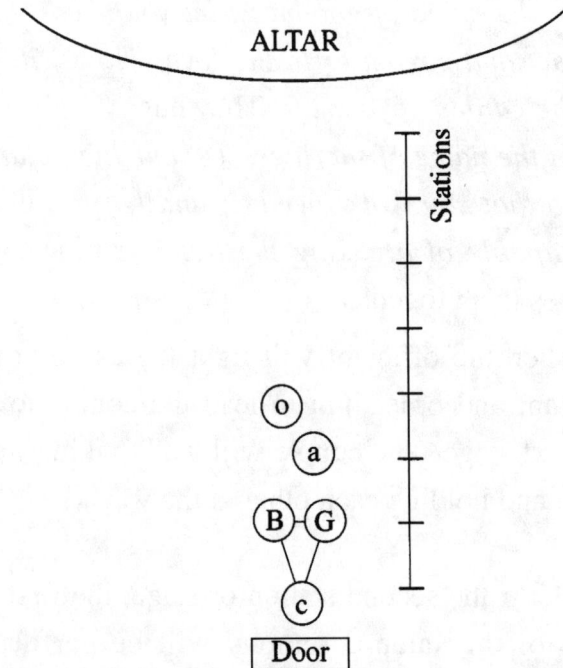

Diagram B, Station 2

C. Then they will start the journey toward the third stage while great temple music is playing. At this station they will pause and perform the first four steps of the ceremony again, and the minister will say for the fifth statement:

In the name of sacred labor, explain to the child your intentions.

The assistant will give his candle to the child.

Then the bride and groom together will hold the child, raise him above their heads, then bring him down and kiss him on the forehead.

The configuration will then change. The child will hold the candle and lead the bride and groom,

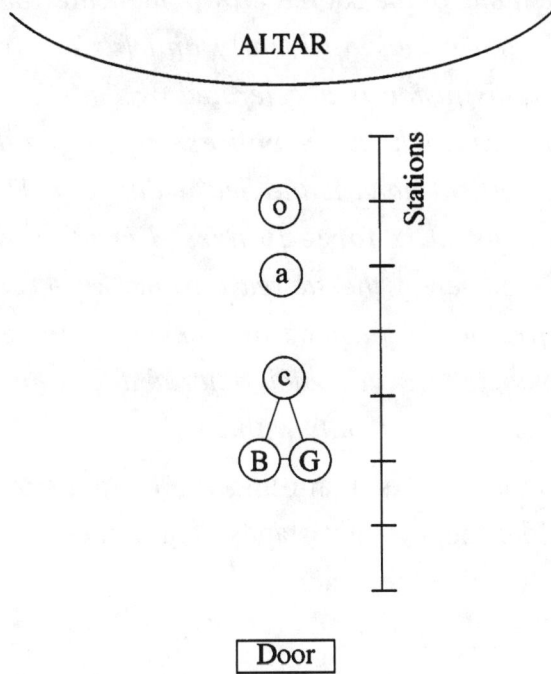

Diagram C, Station 3

D. The next journey will again start with music. At the fourth stage or station, the couple will pause and repeat the ceremony up to the fifth step. Then the child will face the altar. The bride and groom will face each other. The assistant will hold a cross and touch the heads of the bride and groom with it, while at the same time the bride and groom will touch their foreheads, holding hands. The minister will then say:

In the name of the sacred crown, dedicate your souls to each other until unity and fusion are achieved. This fusion is accelerated by the sacred fire of the cross which symbolizes self-forgetfulness. The vertical hand is the Self within you. The horizontal hand is forgetfulness. Let me now invoke the power of the sacred crown: 'My Lord, let your fire be the furnace of alchemy in which these two souls fuse with each other and thus have the first experience of unity with You.'

The music starts again and the couple stand side by side; the assistant stands behind them, and they are all facing the altar.

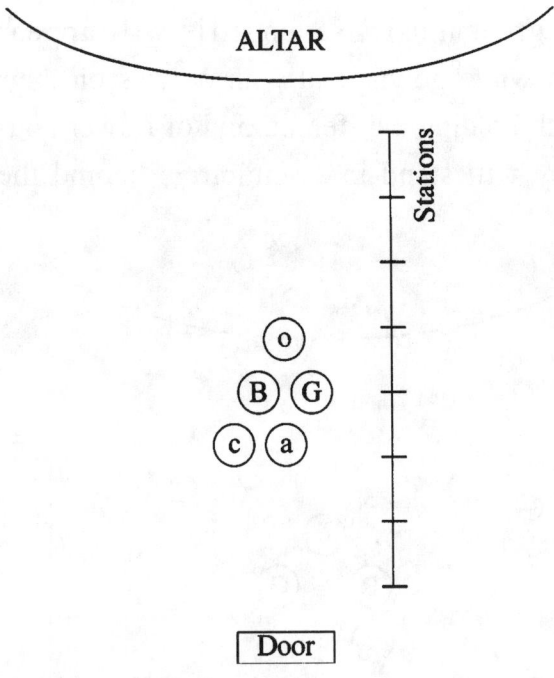

Diagram D, Station 4

E. The journey toward the fifth station will begin. At this station the couple will pause and perform the ceremony again. The child and the assistant will be facing the altar and the minister will be facing the couple.

After the first four steps of the ceremony are again performed, the officiant will say:

The virtues are as lights on our Path. They are our strength. They are our wealth. Let the seven great virtues appear.

With great music, seven girls will appear dressed in white gowns and with crowns on their heads, each holding a different kind of flower bouquet. They will stand in a semicircle behind the officiant.

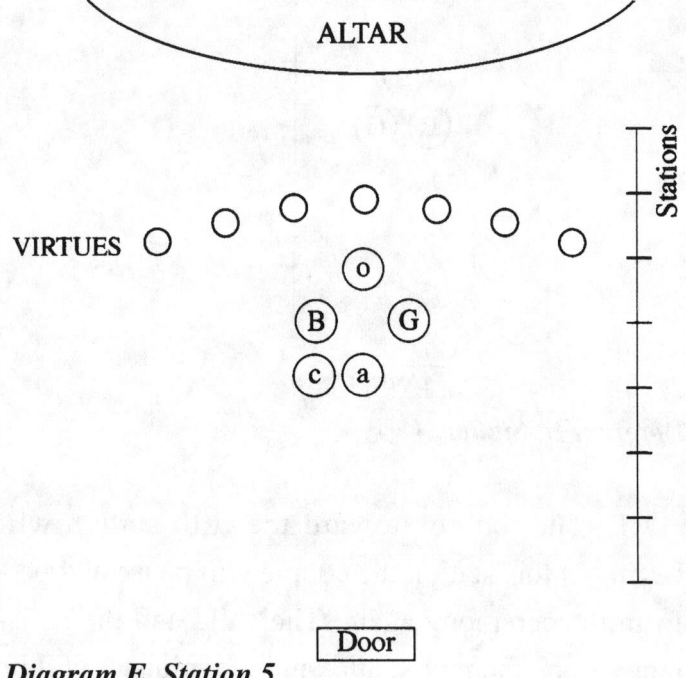

Diagram E, Station 5

1. "Gratitude" will come and stand in front of the child and, addressing the bride and groom and child, will say:

Gratitude to each other is the foundation of the future. In everything, let the smile of gratitude shine out of your being.

She will then raise her hands in blessing and walk away and sit on a chair in front of the altar.

2. "Tolerance" will do the same, saying:

May the spirit of tolerance be always with you. Tolerance gives freedom but awakens watchfulness in the heart."

3. "Patience" will do the same, saying:

Nothing great can be accomplished in a hurry or with an impatient spirit. The birth of great glory comes to those who have learned patience in the daily relationships.

4. "Sacrificial Service" will do the same, saying:

Ask nothing from each other, but give the best you have to each other.

5. "Courage" will follow, saying:

There are enemies of unity. There are obstacles, hindrances, and dangers on the road. Have courage. Strengthen each other and fearlessly pass the dark nights of life. Remember the star of victory always shines above the courageous ones.

6. "Joy" will say:

With joy you will overcome the irritations of life. Joy will sharpen your eyes, strengthen your arms and knees. Joy will make the Sun always shine in your hearts. Rejoice and enjoy each other's beauty. Joy will make you creative, and your light will shine forever with joy.

7. "Solemnity" will say:

Solemnity is a life lived in the light of your highest good, in the presence of your guiding Hand, in the light of truth, beauty, goodness. Solemnity is the power of the kings and queens of spirit.

After "Solemnity" goes and sits on her chair, the officiant will say:

Let these seven virtues be as seven pearls around your neck.

And he will place around the neck of the bride, the groom, and the child, each a necklace of seven pearls.

The next journey will start with great music.

F. After the couple reaches the next station, they will perform the first four parts of the ceremony and then the officiant will say:

Assistant, bring me two swords.

The assistant will go with great solemnity and bring two swords and hand them to the officiant, who will then say:

Here we have two swords, one for you (he

names the groom) and one for you (he names the bride). Hold them in your right hand. Raise them up and cross them above your heads. (At this point the child will turn toward the couple.) The swords are the symbol of your divine willpower, the power of your innermost Self. With the power of your inner Self, dedicated to the service of the highest good and to the Almighty Presence, you will be able to continue your journey, life after life, with victory, joy, and creativity. Hit your swords together and say with a loud voice, "We will do it."

The bride and groom hit their swords and say:

"We will do it."

The officiant continues saying:

Now with the swords, cut the tie around you, and repeat after me: "We cut this circle to unite ourselves with all life."

The couple repeats and does it. Then the officiant continues:

Now take the swords to the altar and place them on the steps, saying, "Lord, consecrate our spirits so that we will live and fight to fulfill Your plan for our souls, to serve Your purpose, and to make You manifest in our lives."

The couple does as the officiant says. Then the assistant picks up the swords from the steps where the couple has placed them, and hangs them around the waists of the bride and groom.

G. The next journey starts, and when they reach the last station or stage, the first ceremony will be performed for the last time. This seventh and last stage takes place in front of the altar where the seven virtues are sitting.

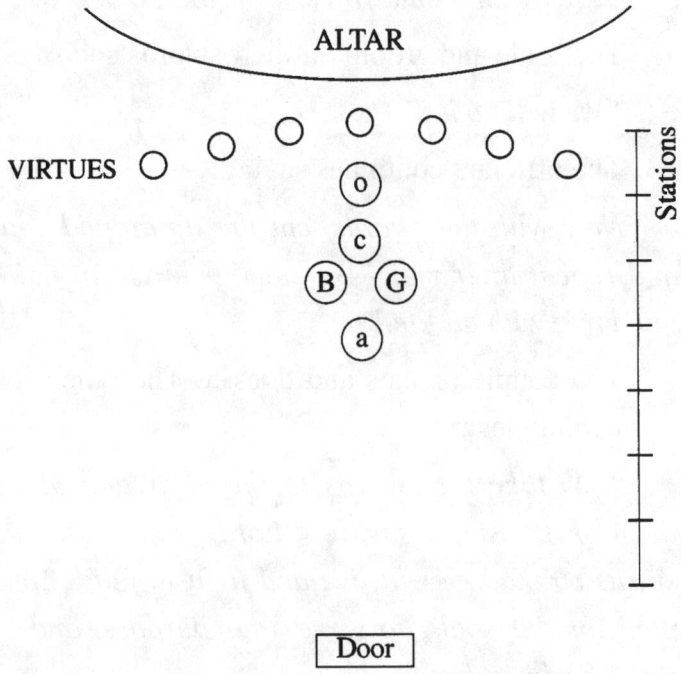

Diagram F, Station 6

After this ceremony has been repeated, the officiant will say:

Let us extend our call to the Seven Rays of the Sun and let them bring the crowns of victory.

Seven men depicting the Seven Rays will come forward wearing orange shirts and black pants. Three will walk in front, the fourth walking behind them holding two flower crowns, and the last three Rays following him. They will place themselves behind the bride and groom.

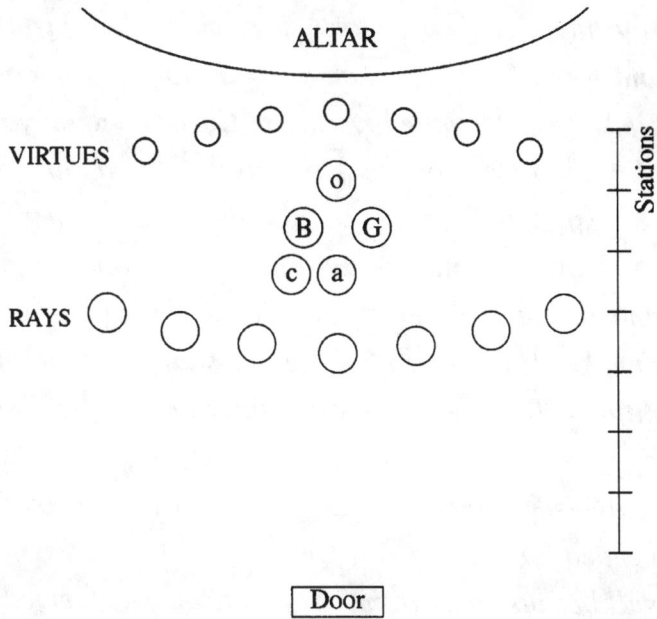

Diagram G, Station 7

The fourth boy will give a crown to the three boys on his left. All three together will take the crown and place it on the head of the groom and then return to their places. The fourth boy will then give the remaining crown to the three boys on his right who similarly will place the crown on the head of the bride and then return to their places.

The officiant will say:

Now, you (naming the groom) are the husband of the bride (naming her) and you (naming the bride) are the wife of your husband (naming him). You have reached victory surrounded with virtues and Rays. Now kiss each other as souls. (The couple kisses.) May the blessing of Christ be upon you. May the power of the Almighty Life pour through you, strengthening you in your life-long journey.

Now you (names the bride and groom) kneel and repeat after me: "Lord, send Thy will — give or take. Together with Thee, we shall examine our pitfalls. Together we shall deliberate our decisions of yesterday. Today we are satisfied, and Thou knowest better than us the quantity of nurture needed for the morrow. We shall not transgress Thy will because only from Thy hand can we receive."

After the couple repeats these words, all ceremonial personnel will say together the Great Invocation:

From the point of Light within the Mind of God
Let light stream forth into the minds of men.
Let Light descend on Earth.

From the point of Love within the Heart of God
Let love stream forth into the hearts of men.
May Christ return to Earth.

From the centre where the Will of God is known
Let purpose guide the little wills of men —
The purpose which the Masters know and serve.

From the centre which we call the race of men
Let the Plan of Love and Light work out.
And may it seal the door where evil dwells.

Let Light and love and Power
  Restore the Plan on Earth.

Then the officiant will take two rings from the hand of the assistant and, placing the rings on the bride's and groom's fingers, say:

I am placing these rings on your fingers as the symbol of your vows. May your vows always reverberate within your souls. May you now depart with the joy everlasting.

The officiant will then place his hands on their heads in blessing. Then the virtue, "Joy," will lead the procession out of the hall.

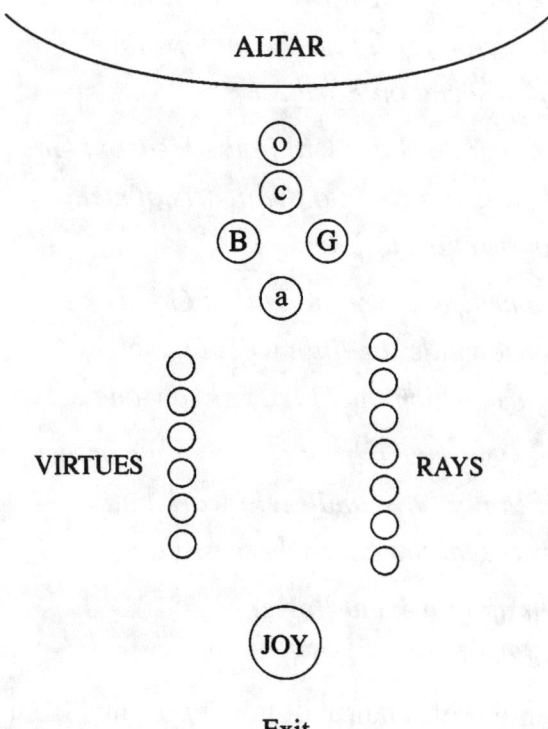

Diagram H, Station 8

Chapter Four

Choosing the Baby

There was a certain meditation given to those who were going to have highly developed babies.

It was believed that souls exist before they are born in their physical bodies. Souls are in different stages of development. Those who are highly developed are called "old souls," and those who are not developed are called "young souls."

Old souls come to work as leaders, talents, geniuses in any field of human endeavor to further the evolution of humanity. "Young souls" waste their time, energy, money, and bodies and produce problems for those who are more advanced. The young souls are attracted to superficial values of life, and usually they delay their evolution by using alcohol, drugs, tobacco, marijuana and by wasting their energy in excessive indulgence in sex.

Parents can draw old souls or young souls. If the couple desires to bring in old souls who will be creative forces in human life, the couple must focus their desires on higher planes. Their desires can be raised from one level to another through meditation, contemplation, and visualization of great ideas.

Secondly, the couple must be in tune with each other, like two musical instruments.

If such conditions exist at the time of the act of love, a funnel is created that extends from the couple's sex organs, their etheric bodies, astral bodies, and mental bodies. In rare cases, the mouth of the funnel is in the Spiritual Triad.

If there is great love, respect, and admiration, these feelings create the right sphere of attraction for souls. If there is disunity, rejection, or conflict, the sphere becomes gray and attracts only young souls.

To help people attract higher souls and thus serve humanity, the Sages gave meditative techniques that were used very privately in some communities by persons in their marriage.

They thought that higher souls could be attracted through the great ideas to which the incoming souls were related. Once a man and a woman were caught up in a great idea, that idea would draw the appropriate soul to the magnetic whirlpool of love charged with that great idea.

Physical attraction alone between a couple cannot create an electrical call into the higher spheres or frequencies where the advanced souls wait for incarnation.

Emotional fusion creates a greater possibility to extend the call into higher spheres.

Mental at-one-ment further extends the electrical line into higher spheres. But only an idea charged with Intuitional Fire can penetrate into the higher spheres and build a bridge of light for the incoming soul.

They believed that ideas are energy currents that cause various changes in our thinking, in our viewpoints, in our relationships, in our creativity, and in our entire mechanism.

They also believed that ideas are capable of multiplication into thousands of ways and forms, expanding into the forms of great movements, great reforms, renaissances, and great organizations.

An idea generates thoughts. Thoughts are the radiation and the network of the idea, and in this network the idea expands and penetrates into many layers to build the outer structure of the idea.

An idea is the precipitation of an electrical sphere in the Intuitional Plane where the blueprints of the Divine Plan are found. The Plan is a great tension of accumulated energies that periodically precipitate as ideas into the minds of those men and women who are sensitive enough to be impressed by the ideas and to work for their manifestation despite any possible opposition.

For advanced people who are closer to their Real Self, ideas are more real than the manifested world. If they were given a choice between the idea and life in the material world, they would choose the idea rather than to live a material life without the idea.

Man, in the higher realms of his nature, lives and breathes in the world of ideas. In his progressive unfoldment he can identify himself more with ideas than with the world of forms. Being identified with ideas, he becomes invincible in his labor to carry the ideas into manifestation.

Months before the date of the physical relation, the couple must meditate upon some inspiring ideas and slowly involve their souls and minds with the ideas.

There are seven kinds of ideas. There are political, educational, and philosophical ideas, as well as artistic, scientific, religious, and economic ideas. The couple must choose an idea that their souls crave and amplify the effect of the idea in their minds through reading, hearing, and talking about it. They must even try to see the expression of the idea in arts, sciences, education, and so on.

Meditation is like the breathing of ideas. First you inhale the idea. Then you have an inner pause to assimilate, absorb, and translate the idea. Then the exhalation of the idea is the expression of the idea in a proper form.

According to their field of interest, the couple will try to inhale great ideas from their inner spiritual worlds. After they bring an idea down, they will brood upon it through thinking, analyzing, and trying to find the inner meaning or significance of the idea.

Then the couple must exhale the idea, which in practical terms means that they must find ways and means to demonstrate it jointly in the same field of service. It is in the practical application of the idea that one can really understand the idea.

Greater love develops between two people when they serve the same idea in unison, through self-forgetfulness. Once the couple's aura and life expressions are charged with the idea, the idea turns into a great magnetic field. Advanced souls await such a formation before coming back into incarnation.

The second important work to be done by the couple is to develop harmlessness on all three levels of their personalities: harmlessness in their thoughts, in their emotional reactions, and in their actions. Old souls reject parents who are involved in any harmful act because they do not want to be burdened by the karma of their harmful actions.

This means that the couple must exercise right thought, clear thinking, and right speech. They must be very careful not to hinder the evolution of other people through their wrong words.

Harmlessness in emotional reactions must manifest as pure love.

Harmlessness in action will manifest as right conduct, discipline, and creative uplifting will.

Harmlessness produces a great magnetic aura and enriches the aura of the couple with splendid colors and hues. We are told that sometimes a couple appears as a blooming flower, a blooming garden. Great souls are drawn to great beauty.

It is also possible that, when some great souls are attracted to the colorful, magnetic aura of a couple at the time they make love, this magnetic aura is not really permanent nor the result of great achievements but just a coincidental event. Thus the incoming soul pays a great price when he incarnates because he sees that the couple cannot provide the mental, emotional, or physical needs that he must have to be a great talent, and he suffers in many ways.

In the *Bhagavad Gita* we read

. . . that a righteous person on the path of Yoga goes to the world of the righteous. He lives there many years; then he reincarnates in a pure and prosperous home.

Or he may be born into a family of Yogis who are rich in wisdom. Such a birth, naturally, is hard to achieve in this world.

> *In such a home, he slowly obtains the consciousness attained in his previous bodies, and then strives for further knowledge and perfection.*[1]

The third important duty for the couple during the preparation period is to consider all the requirements needed by a soul who may incarnate due to the voltage of the great idea. Such souls need special care, special conditions and circumstances, and wisdom from their parents to meet their needs.

Suppose the couple is invoking a talent of the arts, a musician, a singer, or a composer. The parents must prepare the right atmosphere and physical conditions in which to make him or her bloom and unfold without any hindrances.

If a talent or genius comes to a family that is not ready to provide the needed requirements of the advanced soul, the soul suffers and even causes great troubles to his parents. Often parents, seeing the greatness of their child and being unable to meet his needs, experience intense suffering.

Not only the physical environment but also the emotional, mental, and spiritual environment must be prepared before the baby arrives. Parents prepare the clothes, the crib, even the toys of the incarnating soul but seldom think about emotional, mental, and spiritual requirements.

---

[1] See *Bhagavad Gita* 6:41-45, tr. by Torkom Saraydarian.

Great souls impose great sacrifices on their parents, for they draw them into the whirlpool of their dreams, visions, and strivings. Often, if these children do not create responses in the hearts of their parents, or if the physical conditions of the parents are not suitable for their growing labor, such children will withdraw into themselves. As they grow older they will live alone and try to create right conditions for their talents. On this path many talents are lost and many geniuses have refused to bloom.

When the couple is active in meditation and in the various fields of service, it is probable that they are related to certain Ashrams or subjective centers of learning and wisdom. Such parents, being in contact with subjective Ashrams, draw ashramic members to their aura and give birth to them. But such cases are rare at this time.

In the coming few hundred years, people will realize more and more about their relations with subjective groups, which are generally found in higher mental and Intuitional Planes. Once they establish a conscious contact with these groups, then the labor of bringing souls to this world will become a very serious responsibility.

Our political and economic conditions can be affected because of the incoming advanced souls for sometimes they are the creators of great crises or great reforms, but in both cases they will demonstrate great leadership.

If many advanced people consciously plan to invite certain souls into incarnation, they can very definitely cause great changes in life. Conscious conception can be exercised in cases where parents want a child to continue their path of service and further it in great success after they pass away. It is often possible to have generations of scientists, musicians, lawyers, kings, or teachers.

Chapter Five

The Mother-To-Be

The welfare of a family, of a group, of a nation, and of all humanity depends on the quality of the Mothers.

If a Mother is physically and emotionally healthy and radioactive with love, if she is mentally creative and educated, and if she is spiritually advanced and her nature is in tune with the greater nature of the planet and of the Cosmos, then the generation that is coming from that Mother will uplift and transform this planet.

The Mother is the standard of our survival, creativity, success, and joy.

The greatest opportunity a woman has is when she is pregnant, for in those nine months she can impress upon the child those actions, emotions, thoughts, and creative urges that can in the future contribute to the survival of the child, the family, the nation, and humanity.

If she is healthy physically, it is most probable that she will give birth to a healthy baby. If she is emotionally balanced and pure, her child most probably will have a balanced emotional life. If she is really developed and educated mentally, her child will be guided in such a way that in the future, whatever the child thinks will contribute to the welfare and survival of humanity.

Doctors take precautions to protect the physical well-being of the baby. Specialized education is given to Mothers on how to exercise, how to walk, how to rest, but not enough attention is given to their emotional and mental health, as well as to their spiritual orientations.

In the future, couples will bring babies into the world only with the permission of the higher authorities — authorities composed of Initiate doctor-priests endowed with higher clairvoyance, wisdom, and knowledge. Not only will the personality vehicles of the parents be checked but also their astrological charts and horoscopes will be esoterically investigated by these doctor-priests, who will indicate the right month of conception. Increasingly people will realize that the most serious business in the world is to produce a child worthy of living on the planet among human beings and able to carry on his evolution and his service for humanity.

In the near future, special institutions will come into existence in which the Initiates will teach the future Mothers the science of conception and the science of preparing themselves in such a way that the baby will find the best conditions to bloom forth the best he has in him. The Mothers of the future will learn the science of meditation and contemplation, and achieve continuity of consciousness; they will learn the science of protection from destructive forces and vibrations so that the child will have the opportunity to bloom and to come into the world as a real jewel,.

People often think that a baby becomes good or bad after he goes to school, or after he enters society. That is not necessarily true, for while the child is within the Mother, it is she who instills the seeds of his future in him or who causes the best seeds already in him to be activated. It is mostly these seeds — good or bad — that are responsible for his future life. I am referring to physical seeds (seeds are conditioning factors in one's genes), emotional seeds that the Mother puts into the child's emotional field, mental seeds that she puts into his mental field, or the good and bad seeds that she stimulates, which he has inherited from past lives. The child is going to be the sum total of all these seeds.

A new-born baby is the sum total of his past, of the strivings and failures of all his previous lives as well as the influences gathered throughout the ages from his various relationships. But the Mother's influence, while the child is in the womb, conditions him and either gives him a chance to overcome his hindrances and live as a cause or continue to be the effect of the causes of the past.

If, at the time of pregnancy, the Mother-to-be is continuously emotionally upset, if she is negative and destructive, or if she is depressed or in fear, hatred, or irritation, she not only will put the seeds of these emotions into her unborn child, but she will also evoke similar seeds from the child's own nature and reactivate them before the child has had a chance to cleanse himself consciously of these seeds.

If the Mother-to-be is obsessed or possessed at the time of pregnancy, again she will give the unborn child an obstruction before he can begin to live his own life. Thus, the baby will absorb all of these conditions and seeds, and they will become the seeds of the future of that child. Remember that Christ said that when a man is asleep (psychologically), the enemy sows tares (weeds) in his garden.

If the Mother-to-be is mentally creative, the seeds of her creative ability will be implanted in the child. If she is a person striving for purity and righteousness, those seeds will be planted in the baby. And if, because of the child's karma, the child lives in adverse conditions that could extinguish any flame of purity and creativity within him, this child will still find his way and become intensely more creative and pure in spite of such conditions. He will shine like a jewel in the mud of his surroundings and will never lose his beauty because the seeds that were planted or evoked during pregnancy are so strong that they can resist any evil in his future. It is here that the Mother-to-be faces her greatest responsibility.

Of course, before her labor of creative birthing, which is both physical and spiritual, the woman must make a wise choice of whom to have for her husband. Unless it is a wise choice, she could create a difficult time for herself and for her children, and an unwise choice could delay her own evolution. She must not only consider the man's financial status but also his emotional and mental development and spiritual unfoldment.[1] She must use her intuitive faculties to see the real man in him, for it is he who, because of his sense of responsibility, will share her great labor.

In the preparation for Motherhood, women will be educated toward wise choices. Also, they will be taught how to control their emotions and thoughts at times of stress and strain.

It is very unfortunate that pregnant women are obliged to work in factories, in emotionally and psychologically disturbed places, or in offices where thousands of problems cause irritation and depression in them.

---

[1] See also *Sex, Family, and the Woman in Society* for more details on finding the right mate.

In the particular schools of the future, Mothers-to-be will be trained in how to insulate and isolate their emotional and mental natures, how to protect themselves from dark attacks so that they do not negatively influence the baby, and how to give birth to a "temple" in which God will live. This is a very deep idea. You are building the temple of God. What kind of temple are you building — a physically ill temple, an emotionally distorted temple, a mentally cracked temple? Or are you building a temple so beautiful physically, emotionally, mentally, and spiritually that God can descend and live — or the spirit can descend and live — in it as a living fire to radiate the great possibilities of spiritual unfoldment?

In the future, the pregnant woman will have the best conditions in which to live and prepare herself physically, emotionally, mentally, and spiritually to produce her masterpiece.

In olden communities, they followed sixteen points for the pregnant woman:

1. The Mother-to-be was almost always isolated, and special care was given to her.
2. She was surrounded with the beauty of Nature and stars.
3. She was surrounded with music that was inspirational, spiritual, and uplifting. It was soft, melodious, and of great harmony.

4. Opportunities were given to her to attend festivals and folk dances.
5. She was given the opportunity to have long hours by the rivers and oceans and in the forests listening to the songs of Nature.
6. Stories of great heroes were presented to her.
7. Religion was presented to her from a non-doctrinal approach. Aspiration toward purity, goodness, beauty, and creative thought was inspired in her with practical examples of forgiveness, love, and charity.
8. Food was a very important point. No alcoholic beverages were tolerated as well as no tobacco and no drugs. She ate mostly fruits, nuts, vegetables, and milk.
9. Those who visited a pregnant woman had to pass through a strict discrimination on her behalf. They had to be of high moral standards, beautiful or handsome, and dressed well.
10. No negative, painful, or disturbing news was passed to her.
11. It was suggested that she do needlework, embroidery, painting, music, and various arts, or study science and other subjects.
12. Noise was one of the important factors that had to be eliminated. The pregnant woman was kept away from factories, railways, or busy, noisy surroundings.
13. Special sexual discipline was presented to her.

14. Her surroundings were of the utmost beauty.
15. Prayers and daily meditation were part of her everyday duties.
16. She was to have financial stability.

1. *Isolation* for the pregnant woman is a necessity. She should be kept away from various influences that could upset her and cause problems with the unborn child. In the meantime isolation gives the Mother-to-be the opportunity to retreat within herself and prepare for the responsibilities of Motherhood.

There are many physical, emotional, mental, and even psychic influences from which the Mother must be kept away if she expects to have a healthy child and be a healthy Mother.

2. *The Beauties of Nature* have a great effect on the pregnant woman and on the child. They inspire the Mother with great aspirations and give her peace, which helps the unborn baby grow healthy nerves. This peace affects the senses of the baby and makes the Mother physically ready to produce healthy nourishment and more loving emotions for her child.

The beauties of Nature impart psychic energy and greater prana to the Mother's and child's systems and orient them both toward healthier bodies and healthier outlooks on life.

Stars have a great effect on the nervous system. The pregnant woman should be given the chance to walk at night in beautiful parks. She should have time to sit under the trees and watch the sky and to discuss various mythological stories about the zodiac and other constellations. In some countries, she would sleep outside on the roof so as to be closer to the subtle influences of the stars.

3. *Music* has a great effect on the nervous system and glands through the etheric centers, nadis, and aura. Some music can literally upset the rhythm of the body, degenerate the nervous system, distort the function of the glands, cause many health problems and even lead to various growths in the body. Certain sounds can create, destroy, or produce various physical and psychic congestions.

Most hard rock and disco music is very dangerous to the health, the brain, the mind, and the heart. Also it is not good to sit in front of the television and harm the embryo with TV's harmful radiations. It is psychological suicide to listen to such kinds of music and to subject the baby to such harmful radiations. The radiations of TV and the rhythm and the pitch of low-level music may sever the etheric connection between the threefold vehicles and the Soul, and lead the person into degeneration, irresponsibility, crimes, or various diseases.

Women, especially when pregnant, should be protected from such music and instead be presented with soft, melodious, inspiring music with a very natural rhythm. Wrong rhythm can distort a mathematically accurate heartbeat and the functions of various glands. Harp music, organ, piano, violin, and various pipe instruments can be played with great beauty.

4. It is a sacred thing to have a baby. It is one of the great miracles of Nature, and care must be taken to make that baby a special one. In some traditions people surround the pregnant woman with *folk dance festivals*, especially toward the last months. Dance invigorates the nervous system, emotions, and muscles. It impresses the feelings and thoughts of the observer, and takes away floating clouds of worries, anxieties, and small thoughts. Thus, the unborn baby is given the best sensations and impressions possible for healthier growth.

Folk dance festivals can have a great uplifting and energizing effect on pregnant women. In such dances rhythm, color, music, energy, physical vitality, and dynamism are displayed. All these impressions create a healthy tendency and orientation in the baby. Folk dances project strong vital energy into space, which nourishes the etheric body of the audience.

In attending such festivities, the pregnant woman is filled with the spirit of beauty, harmony, and vitality. It is such thoughtforms and experiences that, when rooted in the woman's mind, repel all those thoughtforms that are ugly, negative, and belittling.

5. The sounds of oceans, rivers, waterfalls, the sounds of trees and birds and all *sounds of Nature,* 'have a very soothing, calming, and energizing effect on the nervous system. In some parts of Asia, nervous and irritable people were taken to waterfalls and were made to stay in the vicinity of the falls for a few months. They were taken also to the ocean or rivers to have a long vacation in Nature. They were told to listen to the music of Nature, the orchestra of crickets, frogs, rivers, waterfalls, waves, bird songs, breeze, and so on.

Sound in Nature has a great healing effect on the nervous system and mind. When I was in the monastery, they used to make us listen to thunder. As we heard the roar of the thunder we would hit our backs against the walls, pillars, or trees. They used to say that the vibration of thunder was thus partially absorbed through our body and changed into psychic electricity, which could cure many nervous problems, insomnia, irritability, and so on.

In one of our retreats, the Teachers used to take us during the early morning hours into the forests to listen to the symphony of the birds. It is the conscious listening to such a symphony that uplifts human nature and charges it with peace, joy, and energy.

6. *Stories of great heroes* were given to the Mothers-to-be. In some villages the pregnant women gathered together, and wandering poets, musicians, and troubadours came with their beautiful voices and great music and sang for them, singing songs of the heroic lives of great men and women.

The thoughtforms of great heroes evoke greatness and heroic tendencies within the baby. A Mother immediately transmits such impressions to the embryo, the unborn child.

We will have a difficult generation of men and women in the future if we do not start to present to the Mother-to-be the lives of great heroes and heroines. But these great lives must be chosen in such way that they stand for justice, beauty, goodness, and truth and for humanity as a whole.

Any separative or discriminative act cannot be classified as a heroic act. All heroism is based on the foundation of self-sacrifice, unity, beauty, goodness, and the brotherhood of humanity.

7. Pregnant women must develop *aspirational moods* so that they impress the embryo continuously with the tendency to transcend and surpass itself and strive toward the central Mystery of all Creation.

Doctrines and dogmas are not religion. Religion is the private contact of man with the great Presence in the Universe, which enables him to receive from the Presence the power to overcome the hindrances of life and to go forward on the path of physical, moral, and spiritual improvement and perfection.

Religion for a pregnant woman is a daily contact with the One Life. This charges her with joy, blessings, and light to face her responsibilities toward her child.

At the time a woman is pregnant, she is closest to being like the Creator, for the same Mystery of Creation is being enacted through her. This is why a pregnant woman is naturally spiritual, prayerful, and full of the spirit of meditation and contemplation, especially if she is in a pure environment. Great religious books can be placed in her hands without presenting an argument about beliefs, doctrines, and dogmas. A pregnant woman is more intuitional and sensitive than at any other time. Any separative presentation hurts her feelings and gives a shock to the embryo.

8. *Food* is a very important factor for a pregnant woman. Generally speaking, some religious groups never allow pregnant women to eat meat, chicken, or even fish. Instead many dishes are made with vegetables, nuts, grains, and fruits. Olive oil, sesame seeds, and tahini are used abundantly. The pregnant wife of one of my Teachers used to drink olive oil. She started with half a teaspoonful and worked up to drinking half a cup of

pure, cold-pressed olive oil daily. She had the most beautiful and strong children.

The milk the women drank was generally goat's milk, and also the older children were raised on goat's milk only. Cow's milk was only used for yogurt and cheese.

Alcoholic beverages were strictly forbidden, and it is a disgrace for a pregnant woman to smoke. One day I asked my Mother why pregnant women must not use tobacco and she answered, "It dulls the baby's brain and makes him insensitive, and it also plants seeds of diseases."

Dry fruit and fruit juices were used abundantly, especially strawberry, blackberry, and pomegranate. Also carrot, beet, tomato, and parsley juices were served to the pregnant woman. They also used to boil barley and save the water, which was then given to the Mother-to-be, for it was said that barley water cleanses the urinary system and helps the lungs.

I remember the elders advising breast message with olive oil or cold water. They said that a mature girl or woman must massage her breasts daily for 10 minutes until they are totally red and then wipe them with a cold cloth. They thought that doing this would eliminate lots of congestion and future complications in the breasts.

9. The pregnant woman was protected from various *negative influences*. For example, those

who wanted to visit a pregnant woman had to be of a high moral level. People thought that a morally defective person could bring harmful influences or disturb and spoil the mind, the heart, and the peace of the pregnant woman. They used to believe that a person's aura emanated his character, good or bad. Thoughts, feelings, and habits are contagious radiations that may penetrate the aura of a pregnant woman and pollute it.

Visitors were to dress properly and not have defective or ugly bodies. For example, blind people, as well as people who had any facial distortions, broken legs, or arms were not allowed in the presence of the pregnant woman for it was said that such images might activate the imagination of the pregnant woman and affect the embryo.

There was another subject about which the elders were very careful. This subject was hypnotism. The pregnant woman, especially, was protected from the hypnotists who used to come to the villages; they were gypsies and powerful hypnotists. The elders believed that any hypnotic suggestion given to the pregnant woman would be carried out by the new-born baby — and during all of his life. Also, many nervous diseases in children and adults were attributed to this factor.

At the time of hypnotism, the human soul is absent, and the hypnotic suggestion acts as the commanding officer in the mental body, thus creating a duality in the person.[2]

Many children demonstrate blind urges, drives, and mechanical actions without any apparent reason. They act, they feel, they think, and they speak in a mechanical way and do not feel the slightest responsibility for their deeds.

These hypnotic commands will remain with the child or adult until the person's consciousness expands to such a degree — through education and esoteric discipline — that he enters into his Soul consciousness. At that time the person will be able to destroy all past hindrances and blind commands within his nature.

The parents or the custodians of the pregnant woman did not want anything other than beauty, health, and harmony to come in contact with the Mother-to-be.

10. The pregnant woman was protected from *shocks and disturbing news,* such as death, fatal accidents, lost persons or objects, and all news in general that would upset or irritate her and cause emotional turbulence in her. Instead, good news was given to her: news about prosperity, success, news that would give her joy, hope, and peace.

[2.] See *Cosmos in Man*, Ch. 14, pp. 133-143 and *New Dimensions in Healing*, Ch. 40 for more information concerning the dangers of hypnotism.

Such conditions for the pregnant woman will help the embryo to grow in peace and in positive vibrations. Emotions and mental attitudes have a great effect on the growing embryo.

11. The pregnant woman was advised to study *the arts and sciences* and was given needlework, painting, or music to do. The purpose behind such activities was to focus the attention of the pregnant woman on lofty subjects to keep her mind on a high level of beauty, harmony, logic, order, and rhythm.

The embryo needs the best nourishment from the Mother. Food is not the only nourishment. Aspiration, vision, joy, ecstasy, lofty thoughts, ideas, beauty, and arts are all nourishment for the subtle nature of the embryo. Positive emotions and lofty thoughts add vitality to the bloodstream of the Mother and purify her secretions of various poisons that accumulate not only because of physical reasons but through negative emotions and thoughts as well. Emotions and thoughts have a direct influence on the glands. The embryo can grow best if the Mother does not have various toxins in her system.

12. *Noise* is the curse of our civilization. There is almost no place where one can escape from noise. But, still, efforts must be made to keep the Mother-to-be away from all kinds of noise. Noise

is not only distracting for the mind and causes fatigue, but it also disturbs the electrical set-up of the glands and cells. Cells can be overstimulated, cracked, and split under heavy noise. Permanent damage to the five senses can also be the result.

Memory is related to noise. Continuous, excessive noise weakens the memory considerably. Sometimes noise is hypnotic. It also creates partial disconnection between the physical brain and the etheric brain, which results in irritation, anger, cruelty, violence of different kinds, and hyperactivity.

How carelessly man produces noise in the name of profit and interest. Audible noise and inaudible noise are responsible for much of the increase in crime all over the world. It will be a Herculean labor to eliminate noise.

A pregnant woman was protected as much as possible from noise to keep the embryo and her system in natural peace and health. A modern woman should at least protect herself to a certain degree. This will be very profitable for herself and her child.

We see pregnant women going to rock and disco clubs and exposing themselves to mechanical noise. At present, most of the youth cannot go to the seashore, a lake, a park, or a forest without carrying a radio or tape player that creates an awful disturbance in Nature. This noise mostly stimulates the lower etheric centers, with undesirable consequences.

Eliminating noise increases the spirit of courage, daring, fearlessness, manliness or [womanliness], freedom of expression, joy, clean intellect, vigor, and health in the souls of the babies. Children born without the tension of noise will not have that premature urge for sex or an excessive drive for sexual pleasures.

13. *Sexual discipline* for the pregnant women was very strict in some communities in Asia. It was understood by the pregnant woman that her sexual relations with her husband would stop for three years from the date of the baby's conception. It was believed that once the baby was conceived, intercourse would damage the embryo in many ways and sap the Mother of precious energies needed for herself and the child. This may sound ridiculous to the orthodox physician, but great Initiates of higher knowledge strictly forbade any intercourse after conception up to the third year.

Of course, in our society it would be very hard to keep the family together if we wanted such a condition because so many artificial stimulants in the food we eat and our close social and business contacts keep us sexually oriented.

This is a great discipline and test for the man to prove his control, his patience, and his love for his wife and the coming baby. During such a "vacation," a real love deepens between the couple, and after the three year period is up it seems as if they were newly married with all the thrill and feeling as in the beginning of their marriage.

For the man, this is a recharging period in which his energy is used to repair his system. Physical beauty and energy, or in the man's case, manliness, are developed by those who periodically go through sexual fasting. The modern physician does not generally give advice about sexual economy, but the ancients believed that the five senses, as well as the brain, voice, willpower, and enthusiasm, are closely related to our sexual economy. Thus, through sexual fasting, the embryo was provided enough energy to bloom.

After the birth, for two or three years, the Mother will postpone the excitement and orgasm of sex and will give pure, calm, serene milk to the baby. It is very possible that the milk carries the Mother's emotions and sexual urges and drives to the child. One can prevent this by holding the mind on lofty ideas, creative works, and by keeping oneself busy with the daily care of the child. When the baby is free of such excitement, he will be a child with more control over his lower nature and more orientation toward his higher creative nature.

I once asked the elders of a community their thoughts on having the Father present at the birth of the baby. They replied that usually the doctor or the midwife invited the husband to be present to help his wife during the birthing process. This was a very exciting moment for the husband in most cases.

They said that being present at the birth of the baby affected men in different ways. Some of them did not like it, while others thought it a privilege to attend the birth of their child.

"It is not compulsory for the husband," continued one of the elders. "He is free to attend or not. Also, some women do not like their husbands seeing them the way they are at the time of delivery. They think they lose their charm or that their image will be associated in their husband's minds with pain, blood, agony, or unexpected events.

"Those who attend and watch the whole process learn much, and often their sex drive balances itself, as they better understand that the main function of the sex organs is to give birth to a baby. Such an experience helps the man be patient for sex until his wife is finished with the baby's nursing years.

"Sometimes, though, we have seen reverse effects. Some men cannot overcome what they have seen, and their relations with their wife get lukewarm and sometimes even break off completely."

"Then what is your suggestion?" I asked.

"Our suggestion is not to force the decision of the husband or wife in any way because each individual case is different."

Through the years I saw the truth behind these I words. I also saw how some women desire to have their husbands close to them at the time of labor. The courage, the cheer, the joy that a husband can give to his wife at the time of labor long remains in her heart as a source of gratitude to him.

14. The *surroundings* of the Mother-to-be should be simple but beautiful. In many communities, she would have a special room with oriental carpets of many colors, embroidered curtains, beautiful vases with flowers, paintings, and statues of great beauty. They wanted the baby to be born into a sphere of simplicity and beauty.

Clown shows and ugly pictures were forbidden to enter the dwelling place of the pregnant woman. They thought that such pictures and shows were masquerades of the Divine Creation and distorted the Archetypes in higher levels.

It was forbidden for the pregnant woman to come in contact with animals because of their low magnetism and their form. They believed that the animal magnetism caused nightmares, emotional tensions, and psychic attacks in the pregnant woman. They wanted her imagination and visualization to be focused on beautiful forms, for that would make her baby beautiful and also her birthing labor easier.

In some villages they told me that a pregnant woman is like a photographic camera, and in some moments she impresses on the etheric body of the child whatever she sees. They told many stories of babies born with eyes like a cat or dog. Some babies even had a very close resemblance to some animals.

The whole idea is that if the imagination and focus of a woman is occupied with beautiful and advanced forms, then it is more probable that her baby will be beautiful.

In stationery stores you can buy greeting cards that portray distorted human figures and gross jokes. Some of these distorted figures have long noses, short legs, big heads, and many other distortions. People think that these cards are funny, but they have a very disturbing effect on the human aura. Such pictures, when looked at even for a moment, create hindrances for the evolutionary urge in mental matter and force retrogression of moral and spiritual values. They also may affect the mind deeply.

When a pregnant woman sees such cards with short legs, long arms, crooked noses, big heads, and distorted eyes, she impresses these images on the embryo. Of course, the embryo will not immediately copy it, but there will be a fight between the etheric double of the embryo and the imposed imagination or thought. This fight will leave an impression on the embryo, if it did not already damage the baby to a certain degree.

Nowadays, the Mother-to-be usually sits in front of the television and watches many kinds of shows that often portray crimes, ugly conversation, hatred, revenge, distorted and nasty expressions, and all these are impressed on the embryo in varying degrees. The result is that some babies are born with criminal and violent tendencies, with urges to destroy and to hurt. This may be traced directly to their prenatal impressions.

Great literature, music, and beauty in their many forms have an important task that has been overlooked in our society for a long time. This task is to create admiration, ecstasy and an uplifted spirit. Admiration and ecstasy have an alchemical effect on the aura. They produce a kind of fiery substance that invigorates, transforms, and heals the body, purifies the emotions, and expands the consciousness.

At the time of deep admiration and ecstasy, the consciousness expands, and often life is seen from a new viewpoint in which many things that were considered important turn out to be commonplace toys. Pregnant women can use this fiery energy of ecstasy to charge the embryo with a spirit of striving and creativity.

15. *Prayers and meditation* were the most honored daily activities. Meditation was a combination of thinking, analyzing, synthesizing, visualizing, invoking, and concentrating. It was a procedure to come in contact with higher values and develop virtues.

For example, it was suggested to the pregnant woman to think about, to meditate on gratitude and moments of gratitude. Through such meditations and prayers, it is possible for the Mother to uplift and expand her consciousness and come in contact with higher forces and energies. These contacts will allow her to absorb more energy and transmit it to her aura and thus condition the sphere of the embryo with lofty thoughts, examples, visions. and ideas.

A pregnant woman was strictly forbidden to come in contact with any mediums, magicians, or lower psychics. In some communities, it was thought that contact with disembodied human beings, astral entities, and necromancy was very dangerous to the embryo and may cause obsession and possession before birth.

Many psychics are obsessed human beings, and their influence is not only dangerous to a pregnant woman but also to the average person. They carry destructive influences and can find an access to the aura of the embryo. Pregnant women in some cases were kept in very private dwelling places so as not to allow such influences to reach them. Meditation and prayers were given to them for protection from subjective attacks.

In some countries, black magic is very advanced, and nasty, destructive work is done by the black magicians acting on behalf of various interests. It is a well known phenomenon that advanced babies are always attacked by dark forces before and after birth to prevent the creative forces from increasing in the world. It will be a great safeguard to protect women and their babies from such attacks.

Some older women even have intuitive power to see certain influences on objects sent to the pregnant woman, such as presents, food, etc. Objects often carry destructive or constructive psychic influences that must be carefully noted and prevented if destructively influenced and charged with negative and criminal vibrations. For example, a lady carried a grudge against a Mother-to-be and, knowing about destructive influences, she made the Mother-to-be a dinner and charged it with all the dirty magnetism and thoughts she could. She then took it to the pregnant woman and, under the pretense of goodwill, made her a present of it. The pregnant woman thanked her, ate some of the dinner, and later became very ill as a result.

16. *Financial stability* was a very important point in some of the communities in Asia. The parents of the girl demanded that the boy have a steady income before he would be allowed to marry their daughter. They felt that laziness and living off others was criminal and shameful. A married man should have enough pride to stand on his own feet and support his family properly.

The parents of the married couple, upon seeing that their children were industrious and had proven that they could support themselves, would give

Chapter Five   The Mother-To-Be 119

them more land and even farms to make them more prosperous.

If for any reason a man was sick or disabled, the parents and relatives would also try to help the couple. On one occasion, a couple had been existing with very little in the way of possessions because the husband had become temporarily disabled. It was discovered that the woman was pregnant, and in a few days' time the house was decorated with beautiful curtains, oriental carpets, tables, chairs, and lots of food. The relatives, young men and women, voluntarily worked at the couple's home to equip it with all the necessities and beauty. A few months later, all that the baby would need was brought to the home. They thought that the pregnant woman should not have to trouble herself worrying about financial situations. She must be provided for and the needs of her life and that of her incoming child must be met.

But women were also instructed from childhood not to be greedy and demanding but content. Women were taught to be creative in preparing food and clothes. They were taught to be economical and not to force their husbands to jump into impossible debt to satisfy unnecessary desires.

I strongly believe that the foundation of civilization and culture is the *Mother*. I believe that in a not too distant future, all over the world, special universities will be established to prepare girls for womanhood and Motherhood. And, later, those who graduate from such universities will be allowed to marry and have children.

A new cycle will start and humanity will sublimate and transform itself, bringing in healthy, beautiful babies who will add greater light, wisdom, and beauty in the world. Through such a cycle, in a few generations humanity will change totally and thus develop into a new race far superior to what we are now. Heart quality, intuition, and the power of pure intelligent discrimination will be the outstanding qualities of this race, which will also be equipped with physical, emotional, and mental health.

The planet will be considered too sacred to allow those humans to be born who would make it a planet of sorrow, war, hatred, exploitation, greed, and crime. Man will not tolerate the waste of energy, time, and spiritual interest to maintain a criminal and sorrowful world.

If people want a better world to live in, the greatest attention and care must be given to the pregnant woman.

Meditation For The Mother-To-Be

1. Alignment.
   See *The Science of Meditation*, pp. 99-103, for instructions.
2. Recite the following:

> *Thy joy is Our joy. When the enchanted flower of a caress blossoms on earth, a new star is born in the Infinite.*[3]

3. Say three OM's.

4. Meditate one week on each seed thought given, and repeat the whole for three months.

First week:
> *May I be careful of the gift given to me and make the baby grow in an atmosphere of health, peace, joy, and aspiration.*

Second week:
> *Wonderful is the moment of birth when the consciousness of the spirit flashes brightly and then blends with matter; there are even cases when words are pronounced at birth.*

Third week:
> *Education of the Heart must begin when one is two years of age.*

Fourth week:
> *The temple is glowing and Our Path is fixed. And each morning brings us closer to the Sun.*[4] *Beautiful is the law which*

---
[3] Agni Yoga Society, *Leaves of Morya's Garden*, Vol. I, para. 334.
[4] *Ibid.*, para 289.

permits each incarnate being to behold within himself eternal Fire as a light in darkness.

5. Say the *Great Invocation*[5] holding yourself in a blue light:

*From the point of Light within the Mind of God
Let light stream forth into the minds of men.
Let Light descend on Earth.*

*From the point of Love within the Heart of God
Let love stream forth into the hearts of men.
May Christ return to Earth.*

*From the centre where the Will of God is known
Let purpose guide the little wills of men —
The purpose which the Masters know and serve.*

*From the centre which we call the race of men
Let the Plan of Love and Light work out
And may it seal the door where evil dwells.*

*Let Light and Love and Power
 Restore the Plan on Earth.*

6. Three OM's.

7. Repeat for three months.

---

[5] See *Five Great Mantrams of the New Age* and *Triangles of Fire* for further information concerning this invocation.

Chapter Six

New Mother Guides

After the baby was born there were a few guides for the new Mother to follow, which were carried out by her with love and understanding.

1. The baby was to be breast-fed for two years or more, *if at all possible*.
2. No breast-feeding the baby if the Mother had any emotional problem, anger, fear, irritation, hatred, and so on. She was to be calmed through advice, meditation, prayer, rest, or a walk in Nature. When she felt better, then she could feed the baby. It was thought that the Mother's milk contained the Mother's emotions and thoughts, which were then transferred to the baby. It was suggested that she read inspiring books or listen to beautiful music at the time of feeding the baby.

3. She was instructed not to relate to people who gossiped and criticized or to those who made ugly remarks about others.

4. She was to do no heavy labor and not too much traveling but keep herself busy with the baby and various domestic chores.

5. She was to keep the baby really clean, bathing him or her in lukewarm or even cold water.

6. In the community where I used to live, they did not circumcise the male. I asked some of my Teachers if circumcision was good or bad, and what was the basic reason that those in the community did not tolerate circumcision.

One of my Teachers said that circumcision could prevent masturbation. But others told me that that was not at all true because many circumcised people can masturbate in the usual manner or in different ways. Even if one is able to prevent a person from masturbating, that person can masturbate through his imagination and thought, which creates a heavier pressure on him and leads him into nervous disorders. It is possible also that the imagination and thoughts of such people contaminate their environment with lust.

I continued my search on the subject and met another man who gave me some esoteric information. He said that circumcision is an act against Nature and that Nature is far superior to man and does not need correction.

Secondly, circumcision makes difficult the interchange of energy between male and female organs. The skin of a circumcised organ is hardened, and the sensitivity of the cells is lost. Hardened cells cannot receive the astral energy that is transmitted through the action from female to male, the male giving etheric energy and the female giving astral energy. Because of the lack of such an interchange, the fusion of the two natures is delayed or not accomplished at all.

Another Teacher told me that the virginity of the male and female must be dissolved not by an operation but by the act of intercourse in order to fulfill the fusion of blood and the at-one-ment of the two natures. That is when the two are considered as one flesh because the same blood circulates in them.

Still another Teacher said that the uncircumcised organ has a certain lubrication that is lacking in a circumcised one. This lubrication, which is a secretion from the head of the male organ, is not only curative, but it also prevents certain germs from multiplying. This secretion is very beneficial for the female organ at the time of intercourse. Its subtle smell also excites the female and makes her ready for the sexual act.

Also, the skin is provided by Nature to protect the most important and the most sensitive part of the organ from any damage, as one protects his diamond pen by its cover.

I was very curious to find out what the females felt about this, but it was forbidden territory for me to research, and my inquiry could have been translated as a great insult.

7. It was a rule not to have the baby in the bed of the parents or even with the Mother if she had her own bed. They believed that the baby should not be influenced by the emotional and mental excitements, worries, dreams, desires, odors, and bad breath of the Mother or the Father. Also, they wanted the baby to feel and know from the beginning that he or she should develop independence and not misuse the Mother for his or her selfish feelings.

The baby had his separate room with his own bed and ONLY his or her belongings were kept there. The child's room was kept away from rubbish, old leaves, dying plants and flowers, stagnated water, bad odors from the smell of tobacco, liquor, and so on.

8. After the baby was born, the Father was generally not allowed to touch the baby for one year. He could see the baby and talk to him or her but not touch the baby. Once, when I asked my Mother about this point, she said, "The Father, being in contact with many people and carrying the burden of the family on his shoulders, possibly has many negative or polluting influences around his

body and in touching the baby can pass to the child certain contaminations. The baby, not yet being fully ready to fight such physical and psychic emanations, may fall sick or become uncomfortable. When the Father comes home he must go immediately and take a bath or shower, change into fresh clothes, and then come and see his wife and baby. Such a procedure will greatly benefit all of them."

9. The baby was not allowed to be held by anyone who was considered morally, spiritually, or physically unhealthy. A person who had any odors could not hold the baby, for they believed that people smell bad because of their unhealthy thoughts, emotions, and body. Contact with such people by the Mother and baby was strictly avoided. Drug users were avoided by all means.

In the presence of the baby it was absolutely forbidden to use alcohol, drugs, or to smoke tobacco or marijuana. During the baby's first two years, no friends of the husband would visit his home for the same reason of contamination.

In essence, the baby was kept away from all except those very close relatives and friends, and even they were not allowed to handle the baby. No male, except the Father, was allowed near the baby. They wanted to keep the baby out of the influence of anyone else as much as possible.

10. Mothers used to avoid arguments and fights. They were not to become involved in the problems of relatives and friends but keep a detached attitude.

11. Most of the rules of pregnancy were observed during the breast-feeding period of two years.

12. Most of the new Mothers had their own Mothers with them who would act as an advisor and counselor in their time of need and who would filter any news before it reached them.

13. It was emphasized that at the time of pregnancy and during the two years of nursing the baby, the husband and wife would abstain from sex and be loving, gentle, and understanding. No reference about missing sex or about other women or men was tolerated. Rather, a mindful occupation with work at hand and prayerful dedication to a creative life was maintained.

14. The Mother would sleep in a separate bed from her husband for many reasons:

    a. As long as the Mother is nursing and has decided not to have any sex during that time, it was suggested that she not sleep in the same bed with her husband so that she would not get sexually stimulated by being in such close contact with him.

    b. If she is pregnant, the same above reason applies, plus the added factor that she

could get better rest by sleeping alone and free.
c. At the time of nursing, the quality of the milk changes if there is any sexual excitement. It was also a protection for the man, in that it helped him in not yielding to sexual excitement.

It was noticed that those who abided by these suggestions and rules lived a longer and healthier life, with a greater love toward one another, a love that even went beyond sex to a love of friendship, companionship, co-workership. The love of such people never fades away, and they do not need to look to other men or women to satisfy their love.

In our present time, some of these rules seem almost impossible, but they are not impossible if one is protected from the artificial stimulants of sex and obsession imparted to our systems day and night through television, radio, movies, pornographic publications and illustrations, as well as through some foods.

There is a saturation of force that occurs in close contact. This saturation point must be prevented by taking occasional vacations away from one another, by sexual fasting, and by not being constantly together.

15. From birth to one year old, the baby was rhythmically fed and taken care of, but other than

that left alone to sleep and grow. From the age of one through three years he would play mostly with his toys, which were composed of various sized and colored balls, boxes, and blocks, xylophones, drums, and wheels, or abacuses, etc. Every three to four hours his Mother or Father would look in on him. In this way the child learned independence and self-creativity. From four years on he would play with other children and animals out in Nature.

Children were forbidden to have animals with them in their beds. No cat or dog was even allowed to enter the child's bedroom. Close contact with animals was prevented, and children were not allowed to kiss their pets or hold them close to their mouth or let the animals lick them. However, they could run and play with them after they were five years old.

They were permitted, however, to ride donkeys, horses, mules, and to caress cows, or milk the cows and goats.

Elders used to say that dogs and cats carry subtle germs to the children, creating complications in their health and retarding their mental abilities.

In our home, the dogs and cats were always kept outside in the garden and were not allowed to enter the house.

In the community where I used to live they always covered the heads of the children when they were out in the sun. They believed that direct sun on a child's head made him develop sinus troubles and colds and endangered the harmonious metabolism by hurting the glands in his head. In winter they would protect the children's ears from the cold and wind.

The Mother and Father had special times to be with the child to teach him to read, etc., but always the parent's relationship with the child was geared to developing independence in him. Even the Mother used to pretend that she would not hear her child whining and crying in order to develop strength and the ability in him to stand on his own feet and take care of himself.

No parent wanted a child that hung on to them and cried when they left him for other duties, or a child that was fearful or dependent on his parents to tell him what to do or to provide his amusement for him. They felt that type of child would not be an asset to the community and would not grow up to be a real man with great manliness or a beautiful woman with the qualities to lead a family.

The Role of Mothers

What can be expected from Mothers?

- They are expected to teach the value of life, to teach the beauty of life in all living forms, to teach us how short life is, and how much there is to be done in that short life.
- We want them to teach us the unity of life — the One Life, the One Self in all beings.

- They must teach us to try to solve our own problems with cool logic and with the intuitive power of the heart.
- They must teach us how to respect life: flowers, trees, animals, human beings, even articles or things that are used daily, such as our clothes or cars. For example, instead of removing our clothes and throwing them on a chair or on the floor, we must hang them up nicely. The respect that is taught must radiate from us at all times.
- We expect them to teach us to love intelligently, to forgive and be tolerant without encouraging weakness and crimes.
- Mothers must teach us to see beauty, to enjoy beauty, to spread beauty, to sacrifice for beauty, and to be creative in all that we do.
- They will teach us to enjoy serving, to enjoy helping, to enjoy creating. I once saw a girl who was upset when her Mother started to wash the dishes while they had guests. "Mother," she said, "what are you doing? That is my job. You go and talk with the guests." "Well," the Mother answered, "I wanted you to have a little time with them." "Oh, I can do that later. Let me wash the dishes." This is the helping that must be cultivated in our children.
- Mothers will teach us to be grateful. Gratitude is a great healing power.
- They must teach us to be sacrificial. And this must be taught by example on a gradient scale.

One day I asked my Teacher what the ultimate goal of our learning and meditation is. He answered, "I do not want to tell you. But maybe you won't be scared if I do . . . ." "What is it?" I asked. "Just . . . I do not know how to put it gently. Just learn how to sacrifice everything, even your own self in the great Self. It is better if you hurry and daily learn this!"

- Mothers will teach us to strive, to know, to aspire toward great achievements on the road of human endeavor. Most importantly, they will teach us TO BE.
- We will be taught to discriminate between a rock and a jewel, between a real diamond and one made of glass. Of course, this will be symbolic of the higher values of life, and our Mothers will teach us this discrimination.
- The cultivation of the spirit of independence must be taught.

Mothers also have a great path of discipline for themselves. For the sake of their own perfection, they should

a. practice the art of detachment
b. give freedom to their children to choose, to fail, and to succeed
c. make their children stand on their own feet, face their own problems, and try to solve them with their own means

d. be an example of honesty, goodness, and beauty
e. be an example of progressive improvement
f. allocate time to plan certain activities with their children and teach them how to organize, to plan, and to synthesize
g. never condemn, criticize, or threaten their children, but try to understand, to explain, to enlighten them
h. have times of separation from their children by occasionally sending them away or by going away herself, trusting the affairs of the home to her children.
i. be an example of loving understanding, an example of silence, non-criticism, and non-condemnation
j. show great respect and understanding under all conditions to her husband, or the Father of her children.

Of course, since we are entering the 21st century, what do we need to learn from these people? We have our universities, counselors, psychologists, doctors. They know how to guide us, so who needs these old ways? We know it all!

But somewhere in our hearts we feel that our family life needs to be changed if greater joy, prosperity, health, happiness, and success are wanted. But what are the changes that can be made?

Perhaps we will make a decision to look at the customs and rules of these simple people and observe, without intellectual pride and vanity, to see if their concepts could be utilized in our life, for our own good.

Chapter Seven

The Child

A young woman must not only be prepared for womanhood and Motherhood, but she must also educate herself to raise her children in such a way that

a. They bloom with their own talents
b. They have the inspiration to stand for the common good of humanity
c. They have the health of body and mind to be able to carry the tension of a great service or a great labor for humanity
d. They have a highly developed sense of discrimination and value

A baby is a rare flower that must be planted in the best ground and climate and provided with the best conditions in order to be a shining beauty for humanity in the future.

Some people, after having the baby, do not care about the child's environment, about the influence under which that child will grow. It is easy, perhaps, to have the baby but it is really hard to raise him in the right conditions. But if we want a sane world, if we want an ideal life on the planet, babies must be raised in the right conditions.

In Asia they used to say that the Mother gives birth to her child through her body and also through her soul. If her child is born through these two channels, he will be great among men. The birth from the body takes 7 to 9 months, but the birth from the soul takes 7 to 9 years. These are the years in which the child's soul must have a birth from the soul of the Mother. After such a birth, no power in the world can conquer him or her. In his life, a man draws power and inspiration from these 7 to 9 years of his childhood.

Once I heard a Sage saying that the supreme thing a Mother must give her child is a *noble character,* a character that, like a diamond, can endure all pressures and temptations of life and keep its nature bright and beautiful.

The Mother can virtually build a shield around her child, and that shield is the character. A noble character is built within the child when the Mother, with her creative love, brings into action the spirit aspect of the child and kindles a vision of nobility, beauty, generosity, simplicity, dignity, strength, and compassion. Such a child can be in any condition, and nothing will affect him, for in mysterious ways he will always come out from multicolor temptations and stand always victorious.

I remember how my Mother used to create independence and striving in me. For example, once a year there was a sports festival. Hundreds of young people would participate in this festival. I was in the high-jump and the 100-meter run. I won the 100-meter run and became the champion, but I came in second in the high-jump.

My Mother had not attended the festival, but she knew all about the results before I told her. Giving me a mysterious look she said, "You would have had dinner tonight if you had won your high-jump."

"Well," I said, "my shoe came loose when I was jumping so I hit the bar, but I came in second . . . ."

"I know, but you have been the first," and offering a piece of cake to me, she sat down with me and told me the following story:

There was a castle in which two brothers were living with their Mother. These brothers were great warriors and had an army of soldiers.

One day, an enemy of the brothers attacked their castle, but the enemy was turned back. After a while, the enemy gathered new forces and again attacked the castle.

The two brothers again rushed out with their soldiers and pushed the enemy back ten miles while killing some of them. The battle lasted all day and was very fierce, and the brothers were wounded. The brothers thought they would go back to the castle while their soldiers were still fighting. So they went back to the castle and knocked on the gate to be let in. The Mother came to the gate and asked who was there. They replied, "It is your sons, and we are wounded and have almost lost the battle."

"I do not have sons that escape or become defeated," replied the Mother.

"Mother, please."

"I have no sons."

The two brothers became inspired by the braveness of their Mother and rushed back to the battle and gave new courage to their soldiers. Toward dawn, they were exhausted but victorious.

When they came back with the remainder of their soldiers, the Mother opened the gates of the castle and said, "Only victorious ones are allowed to enter these gates.

The ancients used to call the Mother the "inspirer of heroes."

The Mother must always inspire strength, independence, dignity, and a sense of justice in her children for the seeds of many dangers exist within the child, waiting for restimulation. Children bring their karmic liabilities from previous lives into their present life, and knowing this we do not approach them as angels but as human beings who need right guidance.

It is from the third to fourth year of age that the Mother must start systematically building the character of the child. The character of the child is first built by the *example* of the Mother. A Mother has a serious responsibility to be an example to the child, for a child cannot *be* through what a Mother says, but through whatever the Mother *is*. A Mother can say many beautiful things to her child, sing to him when she is giving him a bath, tell him lots of fairy tales and stories, but if the child doesn't see the principles and beauty in the Mother's life, it creates contradictions in the child's mind and he becomes "double-minded" and a failure. The child may think, "Mommy *says* good things, but Mommy *does* bad things." Therefore, the child thinks he can do both also: "I can *say* good things and *do* bad things because Mommy does that."

There are a few virtues that the Mother must exemplify and, through the medium of stories or fairy tales, plant in the mind of the child. These virtues are the following:

- love for beauty
- love for living creatures
- gratitude
- fearlessness
- sense of righteousness
- nobility
- solemnity

- striving
- joyfulness
- patience

When these virtues are presented to the child through stories, fairy tales, and by example, they will evoke the soul of the child and make the soul start to control the personality and the life of the child. The consciousness of the child expands as the soul gains more and more control over the child's personality vehicles.

Through such a training, the future generation will be saved from increasing crimes and wars.

Some people try to control their child by fear or bribery. This is the most dangerous technique. It either paralyzes the child or makes him an outlaw. In some villages in which I lived, the children were handled the best way possible. They used to think that a child would not need punishing if the parents gave him the right education, handled him with loving understanding, and protected him from bad influences.

Whenever a child was punished, people used to feel that the parents of that child needed an education because they failed in some way to raise their child in a proper way.

Children are very open to virtues because their personality is not yet overloaded with the glamors and illusions of the world, and the soul is not yet sunk into matter.

Children used to play mostly with and in Nature — lakes, rivers, forests, and animals. Toys were given to them with great discrimination. They were mostly balls and musical instruments, or wooden blocks and wheels of various sizes, also colorful beads, buttons, marbles, bracelets, rings, necklaces, and pencils. The children would use these objects to build and create according to their imagination.

The elders were very careful not to permit any representation of disfigured or deformed animals or human figures as toys. This also applied to the pictures on cards or drawings. Anything out of proportion or disfigured was cast away as an unhealthy toy, or as an insult to the Creator.

Our American children are loaded with toys and are so very toy conscious and greedy for them that they need to have new toys continuously in order to be satisfied and happy.

After the holidays, you see children visiting and playing with each other and showing off their toys in great pride . . . their machine-guns, rifles, hand-guns, bombs, various war weapons, disfigured animals, dolls, and so on and so on . . . and if new toys are not brought to them, they are resentful and unhappy for a long time.

In the communities I visited in Asia, they did not believe in such toys. There was no shop that used to make or sell children's toys.

Throughout the years I have observed children who had various roomfuls of toys and children without toys. The children without commerical toys were more creative, artistic, sensitive, and had a spirit of gratitude — much more so than those who had plenty of toys. They were also very social. They used to play with each other and create their own games to play with their sisters and brothers, Mother and Father, and take part in all the labors at home.

Children without artificial toys had their toys, but they made them with their own hands.

At one time, my friends and I had a boat for the river. It took us six months to build it, and we gave all our spare time to it. We learned many new things every time we tried to improve it. Such a labor evoked a creative spirit from within us. Later, we made a carriage and even a piano to play our own music. We increased our instruments to include drums, pipes, whistles, cymbals, violins, and guitars; all these we made ourselves. We made our own telephone and had special signals to communicate with each other. I still remember the special alphabet that we children created in order to communicate secrets to one another.

Those who have commercial toys in some sense block their creativity, their spirit of adaptation and group work, and enter into a world of satisfaction, attachment, dependency, loneliness, and fantasy.

Each child was also busy helping his parents. Children one to five years of age used to play, but the older children would play by helping their Mother and Father. They would help them with the animals, the horses, donkeys, chickens, goats, cows, calves, or help them with the gardening, repairing, painting, building — working with their Father and Mother on vacation days.

Lazy boys and those who used to wander the streets were looked upon as failures and watched carefully by the authorities.

My joyful and creative years suddenly came to an end on a New Year's day when my Uncle brought me a stuffed bear from the city. My Father used to call my Uncle a "city man," which meant artificial or mechanical. That bear was so real-looking that it took me a long time to touch it.

I was very much excited about the bear, and when I looked at my Mother and invited her with my look to share my joy, I found her very indifferent, as if something wrong had been done to me. But she couldn't prevent it because it was given by her brother whom she hadn't seen in ten years.

I wanted her so badly to join in my joy and excitement, but I found her rejecting, indifferent, and unhappy.

My Uncle looked embarrassingly toward Mother and happily toward me.

Later I heard Mother telling my Uncle, "You could bring clothes or shoes for him or some tools, but not a toy, an imitation . . . ."

"But sister, he loved it!" he answered.

"I know."

I developed such a fear about losing my bear that I almost baby-sat it. I became aloof and developed cold feelings toward my Mother, sisters, and friends and also subjectively toward my Uncle for hurting the feelings of my Mother.

The bear was with me always, and because I was identified with it, all silent rejections of it from Mother and sisters were rejections of me.

Daddy kept himself out of this complication and only once he said, "I am going to bring you a pony. I know you will like it."

"When?" I asked.

"Maybe next week."

"Can I ride my pony with the bear?"

"If you give your whole attention to your pony so that you do not fall down with the bear . . . ."

"I will."

The pony came, but my bear was riding the pony more than I.

A year passed, we were immigrating from the town to a big city that was five hundred miles away, a modern city with two million people. I was eight years old. They packed everything except my bear. It was almost a rag, torn apart in various places. I wanted to take it, but I was ashamed and thought it was pretty old. I was sad but controlled and full of some excitement for the journey, for the sea, steamboats, big bridges, the big city, and apartments . . . .

The furniture was on a truck, and the truck had left us half an hour earlier. We were a little late because my Mother wanted to say goodbye to all our neighbors.

When we were ready to go, Daddy looked at everybody and said, "Is everything okay? Shall we depart?"

My elder sister answered, "Everything is okay, but let us look at our house one last time and say goodbye to it before our car departs."

So we turned to look at our house . . . and I saw my bear in the window with his hand up saying goodbye!

I jumped on my sister, and with silent tears I hit her and hit her until my Daddy picked me up and locked me in his arms. Nobody at first realized why. Then Mother looked at my sister and said, "You asked for it. Let us go."

For many days I did not eat and I did not speak.

One day my Father took me to a garden in the new city and said, "You know you are now a grown man. I understand your feeling about the bear, but . . . ."

"Daddy, it is not the bear . . . ."

"What is it then? . . . I know, but we were not able to find a way out of it. . . Your bear sapped so much energy from you and almost became an entity. You became cold, negative, and indifferent to your friends."

"But my sister...."

"Oh, she was using a wrong method to detach you from something unreal that you made real... and do you know what else? As long as you were with your bear, you never came to me and asked me to tell you stories of great heroes as you used to do. Now you are going to start a new school, and I want you to make friends and be the best in the school."

I felt ashamed and Daddy, to heal me further, said, "Now as you grow you will slowly realize that nothing is worthwhile in the world to attach to our heart... except the striving toward a creative life, joy, and beauty...." Then putting his hand on my shoulder, he added, "Actually, commercial toys waste your time, but if you yourself create a toy, you gain time because you learn how to materialize an idea. The best toys are toys that can be used for something...."

Many, many years passed; still there was some wound in me.

The life took me away from my family for many years. After eighteen years' absence from my family, I went to see them for the last time. For a few days there were many relations and old friends who visited me. It was on the last day of my visit that Daddy and I went to a mountain for some serious talk.

Daddy was as beautiful as before, and at the end of our conversation he looked at me with a big smile and hugged me. Then pointing to the sky he said, "There is your friend."

I did not understand and asked, "My friend?"

"Yes, look closely . . . there" He pointed his finger to the "Great Bear." I looked at Daddy, and all my past came to my heart . . . my bear saying goodbye to me . . . tears dropped from my eyes. "Why, Daddy, did you bring it again to my memory?"

He kept silent for a while and said, "Well, there was still tension in you; I wanted to replace your bear with the Great Bear. . . . *That* is a real toy to play with." And he spoke about the seven stars, the seven Rishis, and the seven Pleiades whom they loved.

I very much admired the way my Father spoke to me. I looked at him with great love and respect and asked, "I wonder why you never interfered with the incident of the bear?"

"Well, everybody at home had a lesson to learn and some adjustments to make."

"Why, then, did you not advise me?"

"I did a little, but my policy was not to interfere if things were not critical, or when too much emotion was involved. And also it is not easy to find the right way and the right moment to interfere, for emotions are not easy to understand, and it is hard to speak the right language with them. If too many emotions and too many people were involved, my policy was, and is, to wait until some amount of the emotions is exhausted and there is some evidence that thought will be used.

"Premature interference does not allow people to learn, and when they do not learn, your advice is rejected. Also, it takes time to study people's psychology to prepare the best way to help them."

He put his hands on my shoulders, and we went down the mountain in silence. This was the last time I saw my Daddy.

There was a very important subject on which the elder men and women used to put great emphasis. This was how to create respect and trust in the children toward the parents and how to encourage children in their good behavior and good conduct without flattering them.

To create respect and trust in the children toward the parents, the parents were taught not to argue, fight, or display any disrespectful manners in front of the children.

Gossip was forbidden; criticism was forbidden; ugly jokes between husband and wife or between parents and other people were forbidden.

Parents were not supposed to create doubt in the minds of the children about their love and confidence toward each other. Any disrespectful act of the parents performed in the presence of the children was considered very disgraceful conduct and was taken as an attack upon the integrity of the children.

Anger and hatred were also very much controlled in the presence of children.

The parents were expected to be very honest with their children. They should not promise if they could not meet their promise. They should never lie to their children. They should never steal or make their children think of them as unreliable human beings.

Children instinctively feel the honesty of their parents. They have a pure sense of justice and harmony, and they like unity rather than disunity.

With such conduct the parents used to cultivate trust and respect in the children.

Many psychological disturbances come to the surface as the children grow, and most of these originate from the lack of trust in their parents.

Children's relationships with each other, and later with their society, become defective, evasive, and non-constructive when they do not have trust in their heart toward their Father and Mother.

We approach children as young, undeveloped human beings, but we forget that children register all that they experience and that this registration is more impressive and more effective in their growing years than in adult life. Impressions received in childhood are almost non-erasable.

Trust of the parents makes a child have confidence in human worth. This is very important. Most of our wrong relations with others are based on the attitude that people do not have worth. If we have lost our faith in human beings, we begin to manipulate, exploit, and use them for our own pleasures or discard them when they no longer serve our purposes.

The foundation of trust in other human beings can only be built by the trust our parents develop in us during our early childhood.

Educators used to believe that the good deeds of children should be encouraged but not flattered. Flattery was considered an evil.

They used to define three words: encouragement, appreciation, and flattery.

When a child helped his Mother, or helped anyone, he was received with a smile and hugs, but immediately was made aware of how much could yet be done at home and outside of the home. Any good act was an opportunity for the Mother and Father to remind the child about other needs that were waiting to be met. Parents used to give examples of great heroes or servers who performed great deeds. This was encouragement.

Appreciation was expressed to the child by making him to know how much time, energy, money, and anxiety he saved others by doing such good work. They used to explain that every good deed is done for all, it affects all, all benefit from it, and eventually all good deeds make the life more beautiful and livable. This was appreciation.

Flattery was explained as an attitude in which the pride, vanity, and ego of the child are pumped up; as if only he could do something great like that; as if he were the only one because, "You are our child, and therefore the greatest child walking on the earth."

Flattery is an attitude that infers that the most important thing in doing good is the recognition for the deed from others rather than the performance of the good deed done for its own sake.

Children raised on flattery and without respect for the parents lack self-respect and eventually become problems in society and in their schools and churches.

Respect and appreciation build self-respect and confidence in the child. These are two very important virtues upon which a successful life can be built.

Before children reached the age of fourteen, they had information about sex through their Aunts and Uncles who explained the real function of the sex organs and the urge to produce future generations, if needed. The emotional parts of the story were not touched upon until the child was ready to handle them.

I remember my Uncle answered a few of my questions about animals, and I understood very well. No emotion or excitement was involved because of the way he explained it to me: as a complicated, natural function to produce the species.

When children reached the age of fourteen, they started the five-pointed responsibility course of which the first course was the sex lesson. This course was divided into six classes:

1) the duty of the organs
2) the hygenic care of the organs
3) moral purity
4) dangers of various kinds of misuse
5) control and mastery of premature or overstimulated urges and drives of sex
6) the benefits of moral control

Parents and Teachers used to explain physiologically and esoterically why one should not be involved with sex until the age of 18 to 21. This point interested me very much, and I wanted further explanations from my Father.

"Well," he said, "we have three vehicles: the etheric body, which sustains the physical body as its shield and electrical counterpart; we have the emotional body, which is another mechanism for emotional and aspirational contact; and the mental body, which exists to learn the laws of Nature, to contact higher energies. and to use the will power to lead a purposeful life on earth. Now, in a boy, these vehicles are not fully integrated and aligned until the age of 21. The girls achieve this integration from 15 to 16 years of age in order to prepare them for the duties of Motherhood. From 13 to 21 the energy of sex is used by the body to connect, to relate, to integrate, and to fuse these bodies in such a way that they act as a unit. Premature sex prevents such an integration, and unification of the bodies is delayed or never attained. As a result of this, the person has no coordination in his nature; he is not together. There are communication gaps in his nature, like a machine that does not function properly in its rhythmic and cyclic movements.

"When this is the case, the body, emotions, and mind are prone to attacks of germs or psychic forces; remember, unity is power. On the other hand, an unintegrated mechanism cannot transfer energy properly. It cannot transfer the Light, the direction of which is from the Soul to the brain, and charge the blood and glands. And because of a lack of advanced and perfected coordination between the bodies and the Soul, the man cannot receive guidance. His life runs purposelessly, goal-lessly, and becomes a problem for himself and others. Nations degenerate when the youth prematurely waste their sex energy."

At the time, these explanations were very serious for me. I was around 14 or 16 years old, and my Father put his right hand on my shoulder and said, "I hope you were able to see some suggestions in my words." "Yes," I said, "I will try . . . until I am 21. . . ." Then pausing one moment, I hugged him and said, "Because I love you I will go until I am 24. Do not worry about me."

"If you do that," he said, "you will see how the saving of your sexual energy will keep your mind alert, will allow you to grasp easily new ideas and new knowledge, will give power to your eyes, energy to fight adverse conditions of life, and always a spirit of striving toward beauty, goodness, truth, and service. That energy is needed in your studies at college and the university; without it you will lack physical, mental, and moral energy."

Masturbation is supposedly a method to release sexual tension. In the communities where I lived and visited, masturbation was strongly condemned, and all kinds of advice were given to the young ones and adults to stay away from it.

They said that masturbation is like turning on an engine without oil or short-circuiting an energy system. They went on to say that masturbation also depletes the person of physical and psychic energy. Because of this, the person loses his magnetism and interest in others, preventing right relations with friends, wives, husbands, and the community and blocking the contact of the person with his Soul.

One of my Teachers said that masturbation weakens the five senses and makes a person prone to irritation and negativity. He also said that masturbation creates tension in the etheric body and cuts the harmonious circulation of energy between the centers and the glands. It especially drains energy from the lungs, throat, spine, and liver.

Special instructions were given to the young ones on how to go to sleep. For example, they were told to sleep with their hands and arms outside the bedcovers, to dress in loose-fitting pajamas or underwear, wash themselves often in cold water, swim in lakes and rivers, and eliminate all kinds of sexual imagination. Often before the young ones would go to sleep, stories of great people were told to them.

In the morning the children, as well as the adults, would be up half an hour before dawn. They used to say that staying in bed late generates sexual imagination.

In some monasteries the young people were awakened by music, and then, after going to the bathroom, they were taken to the river for a swim.

They would test the children to see if they were masturbating in the following way: they would have the individual stretch out his arm and hand and then spread his fingers apart. If the fingers would move or shake, then they knew that person was practicing masturbation.

They used to make the individual stand on one foot and see if he would shake. Or they would have him look at a spot on the wall without blinking his eyes, and if tears came, it was a bad sign.

If the young person was always trying to be alone or was losing interest in learning, or if his mental capacity was getting slower or lessening, these were also signs of masturbation.

In some monasteries they had special meditations to sublimate the sex urge through creative activities.

One day my Father and I were coming from a lecture that had been delivered by an old man of

117 years. I asked my Father, "How come he is so smart and energetic and together at his age?" My Father said, "He was married when he was 24, and his wife passed away when he was 65. At 85 he married an 18 year old girl and had two children." "Yes," I said, "but what is his secret for such a long life?" "It is simple," said my Father, "modesty in food, cyclic celibacy, high thoughts, striving, a loving heart, and peace at home." I still see the old man in my memory as the symbol of a real man and husband.

At the end of his speech, he said: "Many wolves will come and encourage you to live a degenerative life, wasting your energy, time, and youth. Do not listen to them. The path of happiness, health, and prosperity is the path of mastery of your nature. Proclaim this principle everywhere, even if at times you fail to fully live up to this standard yourself."

When I was departing from the country of my youth, I visited the grave of this man who died at 127 years of age. On his gravestone he wanted people to read the following words: "To live longer one must strive toward the highest. And if you continue toward the highest, one day you will not die."

In the special schools of the monasteries, the five-pointed responsibility course was a lifeboat for hundreds of young people. But we can do an even better job in our high schools and universities with our modern facilities. The anatomy of sex will be taught not as a trap for sex and intercourse but as a highly complicated and precious function of Nature. It could produce higher results if accompanied with lofty emotions and an expanding consciousness and if handled for the good of society.

Until a certain amount of negative conditions are eliminated in the world or society, we cannot raise our children in a desirable way. You try to build something good in the school, but the parents, the child's friends, television, movies, literature all destroy it the next day. Until the dedicated teachers and parents protect their students and children from the pollution of TV, movies, radio, bad literature, and other destructive influences, we will never have a better generation.

It is of no use to tell children not to kill when twenty-four hours a day they can see crimes and legalized war on TV or in other forms of media.

By all means our children must not use drugs, but many children are using them because we have no means to stop the sale of them or there are sneaky legal rights that enable criminals to sell them.

Until a certain degree of control is put upon the source of these pollutions, we will have a very hard time raising our children with the standards we wish. When children are pulled and pushed between pollution and an idealistic life, eventually the gears of their mental and moral life are loosened and they become nobodies or confused people who can be used for any purpose.

There was a movie in which a priest was trying to explain to a young man that forgiveness is much better than revenge, and to reinforce his advice, he gave the young man a Bible to read. The young man opened the Bible and read, "An eye for an eye . . . ," and so he went and killed his enemies.

How can you impress upon your child the value of loving forgiveness and prove to him that forgiveness is more economical, pro-survival, and beneficial than revenge when he is already impressed by such movies to take revenge upon his enemies?

If a child cannot forgive because of the image of revenge impressed on him by the media, that young child is a house divided within himself. That is why most of our youth are confused and have no goals in their lives. We cannot heal a tree through its leaves but through its roots.

How can we teach love to a child when hate is advertised day and night? We must take action to prevent all those things that are detrimental to the physical, moral, and spiritual health of our children before we can hope for any result from our hard work for our children.

Of course, this does not mean that we must wait until all bad influences are annihilated to educate our children in the right way. It would be childish to think so, but we must carry on our responsibilities the best way we can and not lose any opportunity to prevent the degenerative currents of criminal and polluting influences. Until we do so, we will save two children but lose two hundred others.

When we are talking about annihilating bad influences, we are talking about organized interests that make fortunes through their criminal or violent films, literature, and other media. Those interests are powerful enough to crush any organized effort against them. It is not easy to save a child and make him really human; it is a Herculean task to liberate our children from the hands of darkness.

The other day I was reading about how child pornography is carried on in our country. Thousands of children are taught systematically and practically how to experience sex in its various forms. What are we to expect from these children when all of their energy and interest is focused in their lower organs and pleasures? It is my belief that we must expose these bad influences to our children, showing them how they affect their health, happiness, and future; how they can be lost and fall into a trap from which it will be very hard to free themselves.

We must analyze the movies and TV programs with our children and show them the subtle suggestions hidden in gestures or in smiles or laughter. We must unveil for them the motives behind all such things so that eventually they discriminate and choose their way — but this must be done not in a "missionary spirit" but in a clean, analytical, and scientific way based on proof.

I think children must know about the crimes going on in the world against the human race, not just against any particular race or nation. The children of the New Age must be exposed to the world evil so that they know where to put their labor, but the information they receive should not be based on national or racial hatreds.

Very often our children, when they are left unaware of the situation in the world, are paralyzed morally when they suddenly find out what is going on in the world. From childhood they must see the evil of the spirit of separatism and its consequent crimes, and they must be prepared to take action against this evil.

The children of the New Age must be challenged to clean the planet and humanity of all destructive activities so that they develop from this challenge a courageous spirit to transform the planet for the sake of one humanity.

If we do not try to stop the source of moral pollution by trying to build good character within our children, then once they are away from our influence the majority of them will be trapped into joining the criminal life all around them. Only a small percentage — those who were built in the right way before their birth and during their childhood — will escape the temptations and pass the tests in order to be the leaders for future liberating activities.

This is not an image of discouragement, but an image of challenge. We must know the cause of disease in order to be able to cure it. It is not enough to create doctors, hospitals, and police — it IS imperative to eliminate the *causes* of diseases and crimes. Increasing the techniques to cure the problems does not necessarily indicate progress if disease and crime are increasing.

Actually, whatever good is done is not lost, for one day the good seed will germinate. But to do better, we must find out the causes of crimes, for example, why is this child stealing? Maybe he does not have the fundamental needs of life. And if we provide the fundamental needs in his life, we eliminate stealing in the child.

Who is the child? Besides being the Mother's offspring, the child is the nation, is humanity. If the woman stands for the rights of the child, for the survival of the child, for the well-being of the child, then you have the annihilation of all wars and crimes. When one hears "Let us go back to the foundation." It means that the foundation is the beginning, the place where things start. If the start is not right as, for example, when you begin a journey and get on the wrong freeway, you find yourself in a location where you had no intention of going.

Chapter Eight

The Father

After the child was three years old, it was the Father's duty to take his child out into Nature, to lakes, rivers, oceans, forests, and inspire the baby with the beauty of Nature.

His next duty was to raise the child spiritually, trying to teach the basics of the Soul, reincarnation, the law of karma, the presence of Christ. These were the four cornerstones of every beautiful family.

His next duty was to educate the child in the following virtues:

- courage
- daring
- patience
- gentleness
- generosity

- sacrifice
- service
- nobility
- gratitude

All these were taught through parables and stories which were given to the child by the elders of the community, parents, and teachers. They were taught to the child in games, in sports, or by creating proper conditions and evoking the virtues from the heart of the child.

When we say "Father" we are not referring to a biological or physiological law. One can father a child, but he cannot *be* a Father unless he has the responsibility and the consciousness that give him the right to be called a "Father." Fatherhood is complete when the Father not only participates in the action to produce a physical being but also helps to give birth to the emotional, mental, and spiritual Nature of his child. This is very important.

When Father's Day is celebrated, the most important thing is for a Father to see how he is toward his children, toward his wife, toward his spiritual guide, or as a whole how he is toward God, Who is the Father of all.

A man must be qualified to be a true Father. Fatherhood gives an opportunity to a man to bring the utmost out of himself, to make himself to strive, to make his life a field of service and a way to meet the needs of the people surrounding him.

It is through trying to meet the needs of others that a Father progresses on his path of evolution. That is why great Ones, in speaking about parenthood, have said that the greatest school of a man is his family and that the family is *sacred*. It is very important that the man, in his home, in his relations with his children and wife, passes through such a discipline that the jewel in him slowly, slowly starts radiating outward.

A man may be a very selfish person or he may be very pleasure-seeking or maybe even a little lazy. But when he marries and takes on his responsibility really consciously, with feeling and heart, then that man changes his Nature, and Fatherhood becomes a school for him in which he is learning and changing all his Nature.

The ancients felt that every Father-to-be must go to a school of preparation. Hence the five-pointed responsibility course in the monasteries and communities. In the future, the prospective Father will also have to attend a school of preparation. In the future not every man will be able to be a Father. The evolution of life is going on a higher and higher spiral, and only those who can really qualify for Fatherhood will be allowed truly to "Father" a child.

In the communities I visited the Fathers had great responsibilities and duties. **The first responsibility was that the Father must be healthy.** Many Fathers do not care about their physical bodies. They drink, waste their energies, pollute their lungs, and waste their time and money. A Father was to keep himself really healthy so he could fulfill his responsibilities and duties to his family.

The second responsibility was for his emotional and mental preparation. This is very necessary if a man is going to be a Father. He must be mature emotionally. Loving kindness, patience, courage, gratefulness, nobility — these things must be developed in the man. Mentally, the man was expected to have a very keen ability to observe, to discriminate, and to relate. He was also expected to have intellectual honesty. The ancients believed that education alone could not make a better man, but observation and thinking and discrimination does. People were not impressed by the titles and educational background of a man, but his honesty, power of observation, logic, and clear thinking were of utmost importance.

The third responsibility of the Father is finance and money. Many Fathers are very short in this area. A man marries and he does not have an income, or a girl goes and loves a boy and says, "I love him because his nose is so handsome, his hair is so pretty." Then her Father says to her, "But my daughter, does he have the means to support you?" "Daddy, that doesn't matter. I love him."

And she marries the boy. After a few months a child is on the way, and the boy has no means to sustain the girl or the coming child.

When one is preparing for marriage, there must be a decent home. It is very necessary for the man to provide this. The so-called "new-age" children do not care about such things. They say, "We can live in the mountains," and they do for a while. Then when the hardships of life come and hit them, they try to find a hut or cabin to settle their heads. But it doesn't work because as their own children are born and grow, these parents will be forced to meet their children's growing needs for clothing, lodging, schooling, and so on. And if the parents do not meet these needs, their children will become burdens on society.

This is the foundation: the responsibility of the Father is to support the family financially. He must know the art of finance; he should have the ability to raise a family, to be a businessman, or whatever he wants to be. He must make enough honest money to provide adequately for his wife and children.

I have seen many families in which the man cannot sustain the wife and children. These families are filled with emotions, hatreds, money battles, fighting, conflict, and chaos. Such families are not true families. In such an atmosphere, you are really creating future troubles not only for yourself but also for the future of your children and their children. In such an emotional atmosphere, the children's physical, emotional, and mental health suffers tremendously. And if the needs of the children are not provided for, you are going to put lots of money into hospitals to care for them later. Or if you run away from or ignore their mental problems, you will eventually create chaos for yourself and them.

The fourth responsibility is the art of communication. This is so important. I have seen families that were very beautiful and materially rich, but they had no communication among the members. For example, one man was a very smart engineer, bringing home lots of money. He used to communicate with his wife and children like a bull: "Hi, give me my food," etc., etc. Then he would sit, eat, watch television, and sleep.

The ancients saw how important it is for a Father to sit with his wife and share mental, spiritual, social, and universal beauties and truths about the life. The wife works all day at home or outside the home, and when her husband comes home she finds him buried in his dollars or in his job. "You must leave me alone now!" he yells. And the poor wife, even at the dinner table, looks to him to discuss various events, but mentally he is not there. He is in the dollars. He is in his business, or job, or whatever. And then what happens? The heart of the wife slowly gets cooler and cooler and cooler. Everything slowly falls apart because, we must not

Chapter Eight

forget, that the wife is the helm of the family. So, the art of communication is very important.

It is especially important for the Father to sit with his children and talk with them, to spend time with them. One girl mentioned that every time she would go and see her Father he would give her money but not his time. She was saying that she did not want his money but a chance to have time with him, to be with him, to talk with him.

A Father must not only produce a child, but must also produce a training ground, a condition, so that his child can bloom to the fullest.

People who graduated from the five-pointed responsibility course offered at the monasteries and schools practiced their knowledge. I remember the Father of an eight year old boy who one day was telling me how important it was to train children in certain virtues. "I must give time to my child," he said, "for he is a special gift to me, and I want to see him blooming with beauty. If you watch cats or dogs or other animals, their offspring are given time in order to educate them, to make them daring, courageous, awake. We must also take time with our children to teach them how to be fearless but cautious, loving, economical but generous, trusting but with sharp discrimination."

One day while I was camping with this gentleman and his son, he showed me the way he trained his son. While we were eating our supper he mentioned that there were some wild animals in the vicinity and we must be cautious; after supper was over, he filled his gun with empty bullets and showed his son how to shoot it. The boy did well. So the Father filled the gun again with blanks and said to his son, "When you see any strange animal, first try to be calm . . . and then shoot it. You do not need to awaken us if you are already awake. You will handle it."

That night, while his son was making his bed ready, the Father tied a string to a big ball which was wrapped in some kind of cloth, and he put it in the nearby bushes. We pretended to go to sleep, and 10 or 15 minutes later the Father pulled the string connected to the ball, which immediately made a noise in the bushes. The boy raised his head and in a low voice said, "Daddy, there is something over there in the bushes!" There was no response from the Father. Five minutes later the Father pulled the string again. The boy sat up and watched carefully and a few minutes later took the gun and waited . . . but there was no movement.

The boy laid down again, and a few minutes later the Father made the ball really move and make noise. The boy was decisive. He jumped up and directing the gun toward the bushes said, "If you are human get away fast because I am going to shoot you." Then he waited and threw a rock toward the bushes. No movement, but one minute later the Father made the ball again move through the bushes, and the boy fired the gun where the noise was coming from and then ran back to his Father and said in a low voice, "Daddy, I think I shot something. Get up and let us see what it was."

"My son, you can take care of it," and lying back down he continued, "Go and see it. Be careful. First load the gun, and if it moves again shoot it."

The boy loaded the gun and very carefully went toward the bushes. The Father made the ball move. The boy shot twice, and running to his Father, said, "This time I did it! I think it is an animal. It made a big noise."

"Let us leave it there, and in the morning we will see what it was, but I feel that we must move up on the hill. Let us go." And we took our blankets and moved higher up the hill. While the Father and son slept, I went and got the ball that had been shot, and according to the Father's instructions, threw it into a pit, came back, and went to sleep.

Hours and hours were given to the children to make them brave, cautious, and full of different virtues.

Psychologically, the foundation must be communication. How do you relate to your wife, to your children? Maybe the child is totally out of control, but if you have the art of communication, you will find ways and means to bring that chaos in him into some kind of order. The art of communicating is very important.

The fifth responsibility of the Father is to give spiritual vision to the child. You have read in the Scriptures that nations that do not have vision perish. This is a very important, fundamental truth that if there is no vision, the family is also destroyed. Many times we have seen this happen. For example, a man who was a medical doctor married a beautiful woman who was a dancer. They had three children, and their life revolved around eating, drinking, and gambling in Las Vegas. One day I was talking with him and I asked, "Is there any vision that you are physically, emotionally, and mentally striving to make bloom in your family? If you have a vision, if your family has a vision, then that vision holds you. As the Sun shines upon the blooming flower and opens its petals, you unfold toward the beauty of a vision."

He said that I did not know what I was talking about because he supported his wife and children and they had the best that money could buy; everyone had a television, and the refrigerator was always full of every food wanted. He was making good money, he had life insurance, and everything was in order. I mentioned that insurance would not sustain his life, but he said that everything was good.

What happened? The wife, going every weekend to Las Vegas, fell in love with another man, and the doctor fell in love with another woman. The home was destroyed. Four or five years later, they were both miserable and they had caused their children untold misery.

If a family does not have a vision, that family is eventually destroyed. A family must strive toward a vision and spiritual goals, goals of beauty, goals of service. Let the family be a server for something for our national needs, our international needs, for hospitals, philanthropic organizations, and so on. Let the family sit together and create a project because the greatest love ever understood by human beings is the love created at the time of cooperation for a plan. When you sit around a table and cooperate, you develop such love, such understanding that it surpasses all physical and sexual feelings. Then you understand and sacrifice for each other.

I was counseling a few couples who were about to divorce. The first thing I prescribed to each couple was that they must do something together, a project, a sport, or just play together. Then gradually they would start to do other things together, such as reading or meditating together. I told them they would come closer when they started to do these things together.

The ancients suggested that if anyone wanted to marry, before the marriage they were to have a project with their partner. In that project the qualities of each person would come out, and the couple could see if they could work together. If they could not bear to be around each other working for ten minutes, then they would know they could not stand each other in marriage. The ancients wanted the young people to give themselves time to be together and do a project so they could see how they would work together, and then they could marry if they chose. This way, they could find out if physically their tastes were somewhat similar, and if they could get along emotionally and mentally.

The sixth responsibility of the Father is to be an example. This sometimes is lacking in the family. A man can have beautiful characteristics, even spiritual vision, but if he only speaks about these things and does not practice them in his actions, he is not an example.

A man once brought his nine year old son to see a Sage because the boy did nothing but lie all the time. The man said to the Sage, "Tell him that you know everything about him, that he lies and lies." The Sage replied, "You want me to lie also? Now I know you are the one who is teaching him to lie."

The phone rings and Daddy says to the child, "Answer it, but say I am not here because I don't want to talk with anyone." The child goes and says, "Daddy is not here," but in the child's eyes you can see what is happening. When you are teaching your sons and your daughters to lie, they are permanently and continuously going to lie. So the most important thing is that the man must be an example in his home. If he is smoking a big cigar and his son comes in smoking a cigarette and that Father yells at him not to smoke, it is a very comical situation.

The Father must be careful, for his children and wife look to him for vision. I remember once in Jordan when the revolution was going on. The bombs were flying, and everything was in chaos. A few of us hid in a cave. Among us were a Father and his little son. The Father was about 35 and the boy about 4 years old. After the bombing stopped and the danger signal went off, we came out of the cave. I said to the boy, "Were you afraid?" "No," he said, "Daddy was with me." What a vision that child has for his Daddy. And that vision is also expectation. The Father becomes something on which the child supports his future visions.

The seventh responsibility is the creative living of the Father. Creativeness is so important. The Father must be a creative person, creative in business, in the home, in his ability to fix things and adapt things. For example, the plumbing is not working correctly, and because Daddy is creative he can fix it. He hangs curtains, lays carpet. He paints. He plays a musical instrument. He sings. When the Father is creating, he evokes creative genius from his children. They become like him. If the Father would rather drink beer and have a plumber fix the faucet, then his son will do the same thing. Creativity brings out greater creativity from the children, and only a creative family is a really happy family.

If there is no creativity in the family, there is no joy. When creativity enters the family, that family becomes joyful. That joy is the greatest vitamin for the children. When children are physically and emotionally sick and not "together," it is usually the result of the lack of joy in the home. They can take lots of pills and vitamins, but it does not help because the best vitamin is lacking — *joy*.

In the communities, they felt that if you sat at the table and ate without joy, it would become hard for you to digest your food. Joy digests food and creates balance in your organs and your aura. That is why always in religious circles they would say grace before they ate. What is saying grace? It is the withdrawing of your attention from all your problems and bringing your mind into peace and blessings. But if you sit there after grace and the husband starts talking about how lousy his job is and what they are doing to him, or the wife complains that the son destroyed the window of the neighbor or that the refrigerator is not working, then what happens? Your stomach cannot digest. Saying grace creates a peaceful atmosphere in which the food can be chewed, digested, and gratefully eaten with joy and pleasure and with gratitude!

These then are the main responsibilities of the Father. And what is the children's response to the Father? Respect and gratitude. It is even the Mother's duty to say to her children, "My dears, make sure you renew your gratitude and love to your Father for what he did for you these 18 to 25 years."

Some Mothers have ill feelings toward their husbands for various reasons. This is not to be denied, but even so, even if divorced the Mother must tell the child, "Write to your Father. Respect that man." It is very important that the Father has somebody who thinks of him.

If a girl or a boy projects such an emotion and such a thought of love and appreciation to the Father, that Father will be totally changed. It will also create a tremendous change in Fathers who have not been fulfilling their responsibilities. All Daddies need love. The children think their Daddy is so strong, but if his daughter just says, "I love you, Daddy," the Father starts crying because he is thirsty for love and appreciation from his children. The children must give that love and appreciation because it is not only for the Father; it also makes the family complete.

The power of humanity is the *family*. The small family, the group family, the national family, the world family is the ideal family. A great Brotherhood, a great society of cooperative minds and hearts are what make the life bearable.

A child's respect means to see the highest in the Father and try to reflect that highest in his or her life. "I know Daddy did silly things and sometimes wasn't fair to me, but he is my Daddy and he has also done so many beautiful things!" See something good and concentrate only on that good thing! Reflect again and again on a beautiful quality that you see in your Father.

How to respect the Father

1) Take good care of him. If Daddy is sick in the hospital and even if you do not want to see him and want to let him die, go see him for your children will do the same to you. Go and say, "Daddy, I love you. Don't worry. Everything will be good." Or if he is old, leave your pleasures and amusements and go live with him and take care of him if he has no one to take care of him. You are facing your karma and paying it.

2) If your Father is departed, continue the good things he started. Continue the great visions that he had or the things he didn't finish.

According to esoteric knowledge, sometimes souls wait for their children to fulfill their desires. For example, you know that Daddy wanted that building built and he was not able to do it. The son or daughter goes and completes it. Or an elderly man had a young son of 11 years and he asks his oldest son of 30 to take care of the young boy and make sure that he graduates from high school and college. And the older son promises to fulfill the Father's desire to see his youngest child raised correctly. This is the gratitude the ancients were referring to, continuing the good things your Daddy started.

3) Pray and meditate for your Father. It is very good to pray for the Father and Mother so that they are watched over and cared for.

4) Do not be a cause of his worry or a burden on his shoulders. Many children create worry for their parents. If the child is definitely doing wrong things and causing pain to the Daddy, then the child must stop these things. This is how you express your love and gratitude to your Father and Mother.

When a Father was dying, he called his three children to him. He said, "My sons, bring me 10 sticks." They went and brought them to him. He then said to the eldest, "Take one and break it." The eldest took a stick and broke it. "Good boy," said the Father, and he had the other two sons do the same. Then he asked them to bind the remaining sticks together. They did so, and then the Father said, "Now break them." They couldn't break the sticks when they were all bound together. The eldest tried, and he could not break them. The next son tried, and he could not. Then the youngest son tried, and he also could not break the sticks when they were bound together. The Father then said, "If you are together in life, nobody can break you. Be together, within yourself and in your life relationships. If you are together emotionally, mentally, spiritually, no one can break you. If you are together in a family, that family is very strong and very beautiful. No other enemies, hatreds, jealousies, gossips can break through. You are strong."

Chapter Nine

The Responsible Woman

When a child falls down and hurts himself, he runs to his Mother and puts his head on her breast because he knows instinctively that it is the safest place for him, the only dependable refuge.

When I was at war I saw that any boy who was wounded and in agony and pain always called for his Mother. I even noticed that when they had a very high fever and were hallucinating they always asked for their Mother.

It happened in my life that, because of my religious position, I was called many times to hospitals to pray for and bless those who were almost ready to pass away. I noticed that almost all of them called for their Mother, sister, or wife.

When dark days come to our life, we turn to our Mothers as our last refuge. This is so because during the nine months of pregnancy and a few years of breast-feeding, the child shares all the dreams, prayers, thoughts, emotions, and love of his Mother. The child feels that his protection is his Mother; his refuge is his Mother. It is his Mother who cares, and all these feelings are impressed in his bones and brain.

Physiologically and psychologically the Mother lives in the child, and the child lives in the Mother. The children of the world are in desperate need of Mothers, women who are Mothers in spirit.

For a long time the children of the world have felt disillusioned by the conditions of the world. They say, "Lord, we wanted to have pure air, and they gave us pollution. We wanted clear water and they gave us poison. We asked for joy and they gave us machine guns. We wanted love, and they taught us how to hate and how to kill." The world has reached a point where there is no security; there is fear and the possibility of widespread destruction, hatred, war, and chaos.

Why haven't Mothers followed the steps of their children and warned them at the right time?

A man, whether he is six years old or sixty years old, is a child. He needs the direction of the woman. Why has the woman allowed her children all over the world to create such economic, social, and political chaos in which the governments are equipping themselves with mightier weapons, in which religious and racial hatred is still on an upward climb?

This has been the failure of the woman. The woman, the Mother, did not step in when the air her children breathe started to become contaminated by pollution. She did not step in when the water her children drink began to carry heavier poisons. She did not step in when people led her sons to whorehouses, night clubs, and places of dishonesty and crime.

When she saw that her husband, her son, her brother were in dirty business, she did not rebel, she did not make her voice heard. Maybe silently she cried, but the destruction of the character of her beloved ones went faster and faster.

People think that a Mother is a Mother only when she is pregnant, only when she is nursing her baby, only until her children marry and go away. This is a false concept. A Mother is a Mother until she passes away, until her children pass away.

Woman has biological and psychological advantages over man, and because of these advantages she naturally has a greater power over her children. Five of these advantages are the following:

1. Since a child stays 7 to about 9 months in the womb of his Mother, psychologically and physiologically this creates in him a dependence on his Mother. Instinctively, the child feels that his Mother is his only refuge, his life-giver, his nourisher and protector. This feeling is fused within his bones and brain.

Children, whether small or grown up, whether they love their own Mother or not, are always in search of a Mother, a Mother who can be represented as a wife, girlfriend, or any woman who inspires trust and love.

2. The second thing that gives an advantage to the woman over the man is her gracefulness, beauty, charm, and tenderness. Man has a natural trust in tenderness, gracefulness, beauty, and charm. A Mother or a woman can reach her children using these qualities to influence them and impress them to follow the right direction of life.

3. The third thing that gives an advantage to the woman is sex. A healthy man needs sex, and because of that need, woman has the advantage to influence the life of the man. Because of her body, because of her beauty, because of her sex, she has control over the man. She can use her sex to destroy the man or give a new direction to him, a new upliftment, a new expansion of consciousness.

I knew a boy who was using drugs and was involved in crime and unhealthy conditions. He met a beautiful and attractive girl and fell in love with her. The girl was a very educated and refined young lady.

The boy said to her, "I love you."
"Really?" she replied.
"Yes."

"If you really love me you must not commit crimes."

"Well, I will listen to you."

Again, another day, he said to her, "I love you."

"But if you love me you must not use drugs," she said.

And the boy quit using marijuana and other drugs.

Another day, the boy said, "I love you."

"Do you?" she asked.

"Yes."

"But I don't like the smell of tobacco on your breath."

"Then I will stop smoking."

Then one day the boy said, "I love you so much!"

"Do you?" she asked.

"Yes."

"I want you to find a job and go to school."

And the boy found a job, went to school, became a lawyer, and married that girl. When I was performing their marriage the boy said to me, "She is my Mother — you know what I mean. She conceived me. She gave birth to me. She is my Mother."

4. The fourth thing that gives an advantage to the woman over the man is that a woman has a natural gift of intuitive sensitivity and insight. Man

naturally feels this, and in the darkest hours of his life he asks his wife, his Mother, his girlfriend, or his sister, "What do you think I should do?" And in most cases the woman gives him the right answer if her motive and heart are not polluted.

The woman's antenna extends from her emotions to her Intuition. She sees the end results. She senses the motives. Logic and reason cannot mislead her insight. Man feels this. He knows that the woman intuitively has some answers to his problem, but to cover his vanity he wants her to put her Intuition into logic, and when she fails to do that he feels justified in not following her suggestion. But in critical times he expects guidance and encouragement from her.

I remember I was depressed for several weeks. I was listening to the world news about the threat of war, about the complicated and dishonest politics of the world, about world hunger, diseases, and pollution, and I was wondering if a man should still try to strive and help people, or retreat and withdraw and wait to die.

As I was carrying these thoughts in my mind, I went to the post office and got my mail. I received a note which read:

"Dear T., I know how the news of the world and the conditions of life everywhere are weighing heavily on your shoulders, but cheer up. You did lots, and you will do more. I myself am with you. We will work to the end to increase beauty and joy in the world." I couldn't believe my eyes. She was a simple young girl, but I noticed that a new energy came into my heart. I ran to my car with great joy, and while I was driving, suddenly I said to myself, "You had God. You had Christ. You had your philosophy. You had all your books, records, songs . . . and none of them uplifted you. And now you are in seventh heaven because a little girl wrote you a few nice words!"

It was not the words. It was the energy of Intuition, the love of the woman. The insight of the woman passes to you a great amount of courage and joy and puts you again on the line of your labor. When she encourages you, loves you, challenges you, you receive a direct current from her, and it affects you because of the secret of polarity.

5. The fifth advantage of the woman emerges from the fact that her natural polarity is in harmony with the polarity of the solar system and the earth.

There is a masculine pole and a feminine pole. Our earth is changing its polarity from a masculine to a feminine polarity due to the shifting of the axis of the earth.

Many times in the life of our globe, the globe changed from masculine to feminine and from feminine to masculine.

Our solar system is a feminine solar system. The esoteric literature says that the next solar system will be a masculine system. Thus, even our solar system changes its polarity from masculine to feminine and from feminine to masculine.

Every time the earth enters into the feminine polarity, the feminine principle in Nature predominates. But at times the masculine nature resists, and thus you have conflict, disasters, tensions, and even wars.

The masculine nature is destructive. The feminine nature is constructive. The cycles in which the woman's influence was predominating were great cycles of peace, creativity, and construction. The cycles in which man predominated were cycles of destruction because the masculine cycle is the opposite of the feminine polarity of the solar system. Of course, construction must be destroyed when it has served its purpose in order to make new constructions possible. That is what the man does.

The most critical point in time is that time when the polarities are in *transition* This is the time of conflict and chaos. The polarity of the earth began to change when our solar system entered into the sign of Aquarius. That was almost 350 years ago, and we need another 150 years to see the great culture of the New Age dawning upon humanity. It is during this age that woman will put her "home" in order, unite her children, and direct them toward their divine destiny. You will see woman taking the greatest positions in the world and demonstrating great wisdom and Intuition in all walks of life.

There is one very important point to be considered: there are some women whose polarization is masculine, and there are some men whose polarization is feminine.

When a man's polarization is feminine it is because he is Soul-infused. A Soul-infused man is just like a Mother in a man's form.

No woman is born without Intuition. That is her polarity. Because she has more Intuition than mental development, she is born as a woman. But when a woman's polarization is masculine, it is because the woman has stopped thinking and acting in the light of her Intuition and has run after the pleasures of her body. Thus her degeneration starts, and with her, the downfall of the race begins.

This happens when the woman cultivates her lower mind and enters into the practical business life at the expense of her Intuition and feelings; she loses her contact with the Intuitional Plane, or her heart center.

How can a woman take part, then, in the human affairs if she does not cultivate her mind?

When her training and her knowledge, her specialization and her business become the goal of her life and she uses them for her own personal satisfaction and separative interests, then all her training and her knowledge cause her to *descend* on the ladder of evolution. But if her knowledge, training, and specialization serve her insight, her sense of beauty, unity, synthesis, and compassion, then we can say that woman is *ascending* the ladder of evolution. She has more resources of energy and is far more sensitive to the needs in her field of specialization than the man.

The woman has the advantage to use her specialization for the Purpose, which she intuitively grasps. The Purpose is related to the welfare of one humanity, to the welfare of all children in the world, and for the highest Common Good.

It is possible to lose your heart in the daily conflict of interests and eventually turn into a machine. Such a state is the greatest downfall of woman.

Similarly, when man does not raise his consciousness into the Intuitional Plane, we have the world that we see everywhere with all its problems and frustrations.

This is what decides the sex in the next reincarnation. Those who are polarized in their minds and brains or in their will aspect incarnate as males. Those who are polarized in their heart-soul-intuition incarnate as females. Spiritual reawakenings are mostly backed and inspired by women. All spiritual reawakenings shift the polarity of the groups, nations, and humanity from a masculine to a feminine polarity.

The feminine polarity is more creative, constructive, and tends toward greater harmony and rhythm. The masculine polarity develops tension, conflict, and war, and it starts the cycle of destruction if not balanced by the feminine polarity.

There are national cycles and individual cycles that can coincide or synchronize with great cycles or conflict with those cycles; wherever they coincide there is success and abundance, and whenever they conflict there is destruction and suffering but also a clearing.

The masculine nature wants to dominate; the feminine nature wants to encompass and be inclusive.

The masculine nature works with matter and mind; the feminine nature works with emotions and Intuition.

The masculine nature works with will power; the feminine nature works with the power of love.

The masculine nature is the path; the feminine nature is the field.

The masculine nature demands; the feminine nature gives.

The masculine nature asks questions and finds answers; the feminine nature feels and intuitively learns.

The masculine nature divides and separates; the feminine nature synthesizes.

The man and the woman are just like two feet on the path of evolution: each has its own ups and downs, and each either leads or follows.

Woman's Day

Mother's Day should be a great festival day in which women all over the world make a proclamation of their rights and take action to protect their children, whether these "children" are their brothers, boyfriends, uncles, all male [and female] relatives, no matter what their age.

This is why Mother's Day must be changed to "Woman's Day." This will be a righteous change because in the heart of every woman exists a Mother, whether she has children or not. When we exclude all women who are not biological Mothers, we are neglecting all those who are going to be Mothers in the future and all those who do not have children but have the same tenderness, grace, beauty, and heart of a Mother.

The proclamation made on Woman's Day could be formed along the following lines:

> *We, the women of the world, most solemnly and sincerely promise to inspire right direction in all children. We promise to inspire in them beauty, goodness, joy, health, truth, courage, and fearlessness.*

When will women start to meet these promises? They, themselves must be educated when they are with their own Mothers, until the moment they marry and become pregnant. Those who want to have children must start training the child while they are pregnant with the child. Those who, for some reason do not want to have a child must also have the same education to meet the needs of the children of the world. This education begins in the womb. Mother may do the following procedure:

She will touch her abdomen and say, "Baby, you listen very carefully. I, your Mother, advise you to have a direction of beauty, goodness, and truth in your life when you are born. Do you hear me my baby?

"You will always love beauty, you will protect beauty, and you, yourself, will be beautiful.

"Listen, my baby. When you are born I want you to be really beautiful: physically beautiful, emotionally beautiful, mentally beautiful, and spiritually beautiful. Do you hear me, my dear baby? This is your first lesson, which I will repeat to you everyday so that you, as a soul, fully grasp it."

"Your second lesson is that you must be a good boy or a good girl. (I really don't mind whichever you want to be.) You must always try to be harmless, loving, and helpful. But, my baby, in the meantime you will be very courageous and extremely fearless. You will not let other people misuse you for their own pleasures and interests. You will stand like a lion when the rights and freedom of your friends and humanity are under attack.

"My baby, this is your second lesson, which I will repeat until you are born and then sing to you while you drink my love from my breasts."

"Baby, my baby, this is your next lesson, the third lesson: no matter what happens in your life you will never abandon your joy; you must always be joyful; you must always spread joy. Do you hear me? You must spread and share joy."

"Then, my baby, the fourth lesson is this. Now listen very carefully — you are going to be a really healthy baby, and you will stay healthy even as you grow old. I know you hear me. See, you are going to be really healthy. You will never catch cold, you will love cold showers, natural foods, and you never, never, will be infected by cancer. You listen carefully because I am preparing you in such a way that you bring beauty and blessings to the life. You will accept no sickness at all."

"And, my baby, your fifth lesson is this: you will try by all means to be truthful to your conscience, to God, and to the highest good and welfare of humanity. You cannot be truthful unless you are truthful to the highest welfare of humanity, to the heart of humanity. Drug interests and the spirit of exploitation will stay away from you. My beloved baby, these are not hard lessons. God will be with you if you learn your lessons and work them out."

"Then my baby, your sixth lesson is this: you will be courageous and fearless to defend the weak and the sick, to guide the blind, and to strengthen the arms of those who work for the construction of a new world. My baby, do you see how many good things are waiting on your path?"

"And, my beloved baby, your seventh lesson is this: you will be creative; you will bring with you inspiration from higher realms and be a beautiful symphony in the human life.
"I will repeat these lessons to you every day until you are born. And I will continue to remind you of these lessons until the day when I depart from you, my baby."

This is how a Mother must start educating her baby in the schoolroom of her womb. The most precious schoolroom is the womb, and the supreme teacher is the life, the thoughts, and the visions of the Mother.

Motherhood is understood as giving birth to a baby, giving birth to the body. This is not true. A Mother must not only give birth to the physical body of her baby but also to the emotional, mental, and spiritual bodies of that baby.

A real Mother gives birth to the body and the visions of her baby. And when the baby grows, the Mother watches her baby's steps.

The second proclamation of woman will be:

We, the women of the world, most solemnly and sincerely promise to prevent crime as much as we can.

When the child goes to school and eventually enters society, the Mother will still watch over him. And if she sees that her son is misled, she will invite him to her room and say, "My son, you are 35, and you are not a baby, but I feel sorry and hurt because of the life you are living. I don't approve of the way you make money. I do not like your manners toward your wife and friends; you are bringing shame to me. I want you to strengthen your steps."

If the Mother stands in this way we will have a different world.

One day a teenage girl told me, "Every evening my Mother gives me 5 or 10 dollars and says, 'Take a friend and go to a movie. Don't come back until ten o'clock.' And I know why!"

"Why?" I asked.

"Because her boyfriend comes, and they want to have a good time without me, and I am sick of it."

There are thousands like this girl thrown to the winds.

A real woman follows the path of her children. She does not plan their lives; she does not rule their lives; she does not force her will upon them, but she inspires them toward honesty, goodness, purity, beauty, and sacrifice. When a woman knows that her son or husband is in a dishonest business, she will never tolerate it.

She will express disagreement through her graceful and meaningful talks, and if he continues to live by dishonest means, she will let him know that she stands for honesty and she does not want to be burdened by his evil deeds.

I was invited to a Thanksgiving dinner, and the family of the hostess was there with a few of their friends.

As we were ready to eat, one of her sons who had been absent from the home came and wanted to kiss his Mother. The Mother pushed him away and said, "I did not invite you; why did you come?"

"Well, Mother, it is Thanksgiving."

"There is no Thanksgiving for those who live in a dishonest way. As long as you sell marijuana, you cannot enter this home. I want you to leave."

"But I am not using any, Mother."

"I know, but you are destroying the lives of many children. They are also my children."

"Well, Mother, I understand your anger. I am also not happy with what I am doing. I will promise to stop it."

"Do you mean it?" said the Mother, approaching him and looking directly into his eyes.

"Yes, I mean it."

Then she hugged him with tears in her eyes and said, "Today we will have the best Thanksgiving dinner. Let us say grace."

The third proclamation of woman will be:

> *We, the women of the world, most sincerely and honestly promise to inspire our children, our husbands, and brothers with the sense of dignity, solemnity, righteousness, forgiveness, compassion, and the spirit of progressive breakthroughs in all fields of human endeavor.*

Behind every responsible man — whether he is the president of a nation or a group of scientists — must stand a Mother, a Sister, or a Wife to inspire him with dignity, solemnity, and compassion.

The woman in the New Age must expand her field of interest and make her influence felt in all human endeavors, shining among men as a principle of beauty, goodness, joy, harmony, and unity.

The fourth proclamation of woman will be:

> *We, the women of the world, most solemnly and sincerely promise to inspire our children to protect the sick and help the weak ones by every means.*

The new-age children will be inspired by the spirit of service and sacrifice rather than by the spirit of self-interest and competition or exploitation.

The fifth proclamation of woman will be:

> *We, the women of the world, must educate and train ourselves to attain higher positions in the world and demonstrate an example of leadership based on the following principles:*
>
> *1. The sons of men are one.*
> *2. The planet is a living entity, and it must be protected from pollution.*
> *3. The problems of the world must be solved not by war but with the light of the spirit.*
> *4. The children of the world must be taught about the fact of one humanity.*
> *5. Right human relationship, goodwill, and sharing must prevail.*

Armed with these five principles and proclamations, the women of the world will create a new age of unity, sanity, beauty, and creative living.

"By their own hands women of all races and beliefs will help to mold the steps of evolution. There should be no delay!"[1]

"You will encounter two types of opponents of equal rights — one, an admirer of the rule of the harem, who says that age-old customs should not be disturbed; the other, indignant at the past, will demand supremacy for herself in everything. Both will be remote from evolution.

"It is impermissible to drag past offenses into the future. It is impermissible also to preserve the ossification of an outworn way of life. It is impermissible to erect obstacles to free cognition. Affirmation of true equality of rights might better be called full rights. The obligations attending the recognition of full equality will liberate life from coarse customs, from foul speech, from falsehood, from dusty routine. But the new evolution must be begun early in life if thoughts about it have not flashed out independently.

"One may perceive that at present there are many women who perfectly understand the significance of full rights. They may be relied upon throughout the world."[2]

---

[1] Agni Yoga Society, *Aum*, para. 416.
[2] *Ibid.*, para. 417.

Chapter Ten

Education and the Child

The new-age education deals with the causes more than the effects. Our old education deals with the effects, and almost misses the causes. For example, in most of our history books, you see the outer phenomena, the result, you do not see the cause, the deep-seated psychological or spiritual cause.

In the old schools we used to memorize or learn a national or religious catechism. In the new schools we are challenged to be self-actualized, to think, and to be creative. We tell the child not to imitate his elders but be his own beauty, to choose, to discriminate, and try not to memorize but think. The child is not to be a reflector but a source of influence of his own.

Many people ask when a child's formal education should begin. One can teach a child even before he is actually born. Education must start as early as possible, and you must know how to adapt the education to his psychological age. Problems arise when you do not give the right dosage to the right age. One can start at any age as long as the education of the child is on a gradient scale; then the children learn without conscious effort. They learn how to talk at the age of two without taking language lessons. They learn by examples, through games, by observation. Too much memorization and repetition restrains the brain cells of the children and creates mental patterns in them, and then they are forced to retain these patterns and memorization without their willingness. Such a way of teaching is an imposition on them. We are imposing things upon them and their tiny mechanisms, and the reaction may come later in the form of rejection or carelessness.

We must try to create games and projects in which they learn to cooperate and respect each other and also learn how to discipline their bodies, emotions, tongues, and minds.

Children enjoy disciplining themselves; they like hardship, labor, striving, service. Even if some of them do not, we must create those conditions in which they choose and want to discipline themselves to love hardship, labor, striving, and service.

We can do exercises with the children at different times — not to speak for a few hours, or a whole day, not to eat lunch, to feel joyful the whole day, not to use any negative word, feeling, or thought, or to sit or stand for awhile without moving. We can teach them various games in which they develop an intense concentration that can be used later in their higher education.

Reading and writing can be taught to children through games. For example, I put the alphabet letters on each child — he is A, she is B, she is D, he is S, and so on. A few months later I saw that they knew each other's letters and thus the whole alphabet. They learned by themselves, and once I found out that they knew the characters, I created a game for them to compose words. For example, I said to them, "Let us form the word *Love*." — so L came, O came, V came, and E came, and they formed the word. Of course the children made marvelous and very comical mistakes, but eventually they did it. Once they were able to form a few words I let them go play, but to my amazement I saw that all during the day they were trying to form words. In the same manner we formed sentences, and in comparison with other schools our children were far more advanced because they learned and we did not teach; we created the proper conditions for them to teach themselves. We also created dances and movements to teach arithmetic and so on.

We were very smart to take religion out of the schools, but we failed to demonstrate ideals to the children through our lives and relationships; this is what is lacking in most of the schools, not religion.

A Teacher's life must be an exemplification of moral and spiritual achievements. Many times we have failed not because of lack of religion but because of lack of example.

We can raise the spiritual standards of our children by showing them the beauty of Nature, the beauty of animals, the beauty of flowers and trees, the beauty of arts, and the radiance of great servers of humanity. We can teach them one humanity, one world. We can teach them about the beauty of service and let them choose their own way of expressing beauty in their life. We should not make them bloom as roses if they are lilies. If we force them, they will lose their destiny.

New-age Teachers must separate themselves from obsolete ways and means, from obsolete dogmas and doctrines, obsolete religions and politics, and think in terms of one humanity and one world, in terms of the New Age upon us. Some of our new-age children are in favor of this concept, and they want to create a new world that is not inspired by the old one. That is the hardest thing to do, but it is the only path to the New Age.

It is very unfortunate that religions and schools have become the storages of the past instead of engineering offices to plan for the future, for the future life of humanity as a whole.

The children of the communities I visited were encouraged to go to school but were not forced to go. Schools were for those who really wanted to study. Those children who did not attend school were divided into four categories. The first category consisted of those who had some health or psychological problems. These problems were carefully taken care of, and often the child then felt a great urge to learn and study.

The second category consisted of those children who were very interested in the arts, crafts, businesses, and trades, such as that of a carpenter, ironsmith, goldsmith, construction or farm worker, shoemaker, tailor, etc. These children were very successful in their careers, and most of them had private teachers to teach them the necessary things for the management of the business or trade.

The third category consisted of those children who were healthy but had some urge to hate authority. They wanted to live an independent life, keeping themselves by way of robbery and various other crimes. Those children who fell into crimes were warned two times, and if it happened a third time they were punished severely. Usually they would not be allowed to live in the community. In most cases the elders investigated the cause of the ill behavior, and then educational or disciplinary steps were taken to prevent any repetition of such behavior.

The fourth category consisted of those children who did not have the ways or means or conditions to carry on their schooling properly. For example, a Father, being poor, needed his child to assist him in his work. In such cases, if the child was quite intelligent and smart, some rich people would help the parents who would then release the child for schooling. Or if the child had no money for higher education, loans were given to him or her by these same rich people. It was a great honor for these rich lawyers, doctors, businessmen, etc. to send some needy children to higher education with their contributions. Often a doctor or a businessman cared for three or more children's higher education expenses. These children were received in the community with high honors, and after they were established in their work, they would pay back the help that they had received from their benefactors by sending other children to higher education.

All children were kept busy. The elders used to say that when one does not work it is a great waste for the community. Man is a source of energy, and the energy must not be wasted but used. I remember one summer vacation, a city organized 2000 school children to plant a forest of trees, build bridges, and pave streets for the city.

Children used to work with their Fathers or relatives at their places of business starting when they were ten years old. Of course, they were given work according to their age. I saw children 12 to 14 years old who were very smart and expert managers in different departments of work and were able to handle the work in the absence of their Fathers.

The female children who did not want to go to school were educated in the fine arts: decorating, needlework, tailoring, manufacturing various art objects, basket making, and so on. They were also accountants, hospital workers, or employees in various other fields. Some of them took private lessons in music, painting, and dancing. Forced schooling was not believed in.

Years later when I was the principal of a small school of several hundred children, we often discussed this matter of forced schooling with the parents and with people of advanced education and position. The general idea was this:

1. Forced schooling prevents the child's drive to bloom, unfold, and search, and instead he or she develops a rejection to learning that lasts for a lifetime.

Some very advanced leaders and men of great service in their countries were those who never went to school in their childhood, but after working in various fields, they saw the need for education and went to school when they were 18 or 20, even 30 and older, and in a few years they learned the things they needed.

2. The children must strive toward higher education not because they are forced by the interest of money and position but by the urge to know and to serve. The life-energy is distorted and used for

selfish ends when a child is forced to go ahead in his schooling instead of following his inner direction.

3. They believed that a child is an individual, and it is his free will to decide whether to go to school or not.

4. They believed that systematized schooling eventually will create a generation that will act as a machine in the hands of those who are in certain positions where they can manipulate that generation. In unforced education, people develop their own line of thought, their own life direction, their own beliefs and attitudes toward certain values or principles. Forced schooling takes away the spirit of individuality and makes a man an item of mass production.

5. They believed that it is a waste of time to create a hash of all knowledge and data and force it into the brains of children if they are not interested in it. Only interest was encouraged. They used to say that interest is the leader of the destiny, and the destiny must not be violated.

Forced schooling prematurely develops the mind before the soul has developed. As a result of this, education is used to exploit people instead of serving people.

6. They believed that for every individual the life presents an opportunity to unfold and expand the consciousness. They firmly believed that schools were not the only way to expand the consciousness and develop talents.

Some great leaders of certain nations and humanity were not graduated from schools, and perhaps because of that their originality was protected to a great extent.

Schools with established ways of teaching and obsolete knowledge and techniques could destroy, prevent, or delay the natural blooming and creative talents of the child. They used to think that a talent must first of all express itself and then be assisted in keeping its originality, without imposition of artificiality.

7. They often would say that Nature and its talents must not be put into artificial molds. Any forceful action on the soul of the child to develop faster and in a direction where he does not have real interest causes degeneration in him and makes him a problem for the society.

8. They believed that the individuality, the originality of the child was the most beautiful gift of Nature. This originality and individuality are lost when a child is forced to go to school and be exposed to thousands of influences that he is not yet ready for or needing. They often educated their

children at home and with private teachers when they saw a great blooming talent in them, but they never forced the children to go to school.

If the child refused to go to school, the parents wanted to know why. Sometimes it was because another child was causing trouble for their own youngster, or their child hated the teacher or the atmosphere for some reason. These reasons were carefully examined and solved if possible, but never were the children forced to go to school. They used to say that forced education creates negative results. At 15 or 16 years of age, the children were totally free to decide for themselves to continue with school or to leave it and go and dedicate their time to their Father's work or learn different arts or trades.

Actually the homes were little schools for the children, for they were able to take part in almost all the activities and were also challenged to know more and be more.

At 15 to 18 years of age, the children were already prepared to take care of themselves. They were useful members of society; they had their pride and their dignity; they knew their goals. And if they wanted to go ahead, the schools were open to them.

Thus, the schools were not crowded, and the energy of those who were not schooled was used intelligently, in every department of labor and craft. Everyone was busy and had a goal and interests.

The schools would drop any child who could not make a grade of 80 percent. They would encourage these children to go and learn a business, trade, or craft so that they could support themselves.

Welfare was not encouraged at all. Those who wanted to meet their needs had to work. If a beggar came from another village or city, he could not obtain any money or food unless he worked. On the other hand, the sick and disabled people were cared for by special philanthropic groups.

Individual property was considered sacred, and if a woman left her purse near a fountain, you could find it in the same place a month later.

Once I asked a Teacher, " Why is the morality of this community so great?" He gave many reasons:

1. Greed is not tolerated.
2. Exploitation in any form is forbidden.
3. There is no forced education.
4. Heart qualities are respected more than academic degrees or wealth.
5. The children's minds are not forced by any special subject that they do not need or want.
6. Families are formed on the strong foundation of morals and on the sense of responsibility.
7. Mothers know how to be examples to their families and evoke respect.
8. There is an absence of religious fanaticism and exploitation.

9. The way we elect our leaders prevents future complications.

The beauty seen in children, in men and women, is the blossom of the beauty emanating from their Mothers. I had an experience concerning this fact when I was principal of a private high school. I noticed that the most beautiful boys and girls came from beautiful homes and from beautiful Mothers. This beauty wasn't just physical. It was emotional and mental beauty as well. Their Mothers were a source of continuous inspiration, courage, and joy.

Those who had problems and difficulties in their classes were reflecting the conditions in their homes. Whenever a student was brought to me for counseling, I would see the Mother in private first and then in the presence of the student. I wanted to find the root of the problem. In most cases the problems of the children originated from the parents and especially from the Mothers. In most cases the cause of the problem was the Mother, either directly or indirectly. I worked with the parents to correct the children and had great success.

Once a month I invited the Mothers of the problem children to the school and presented them with the problems of the children and explained to them how these problems could have originated from the parents, and especially from the Mothers, and what they could do to work out and solve the problems. It was very interesting to see that the Mothers knew this and they, themselves, were able to present many solutions.

The leadership of the Asian communities I visited was formed of those who were highly educated and highly cultivated in the experiences of life. Their goal was to provide the opportunity for all people to grow and prosper. Any act or intention to exploit the public or to use an office for material interests or bribery was considered the biggest crime.

Once a city elected as its mayor a man who had not graduated from any school. In a conversation with an elderly gentleman, I remarked that the mayor had no diplomas. The elderly man answered, "The greatest certificate or diploma a man can have is, first of all, his pure motive, secondly, his experience, and thirdly, his ability to observe and discriminate."

That mayor was in his office from 5 am to 7 pm every day; some of his assistants were highly educated men with degrees. He served his community until he died. On his gravestone was written, "A great man is the artwork of the individual labor of the man himself."

The leaders were those people who were not paid at all, for it was an honor and not a competitive fight to be elected a leader. One could be elected to office if he did not need money and was totally self-sufficient and satisfied with what he had. The leader was coming into office with only the intention to serve. These leaders were very successful people and were loved by the community for their philanthropic works and morality.

The leaders were retired people. Retirement was not a condition of aging but a condition of being self-sufficient and content, which could happen after a man fulfilled his obligations and was satisfied with what he had. Some of the people used to retire when they were 40 or 50 years old.

After 50 years of age, if the man had provided a good income and future for his family, he would prepare himself for the "journey of eternity." It was after retirement that many people withdrew from society and dedicated themselves to a spiritual life. Most of these men or women would enter into the sacred brotherhoods, monasteries, or convents to learn meditation,[1] the act of continuity of consciousness, and the mystery of the soul and immortality. They would prepare themselves to be able to pass away with the awareness of higher contacts and dedicate their lives to God. Some of them would live the "double life of discipleship," being men and women of dedication to higher spiritual education and also men and women of higher office in the community.

---

[1] See *The Science of Becoming Oneself*, Ch. 18, for more information.

There was another very interesting custom. The children were trained at home to speak only when needed. The parents used to say that a wasted word is wasted energy, and nothing distorts the mind more easily than words used without purpose or for babbling and yakking. When an individual was much too talkative, people would consider him or her empty of real values or full of dishonest motives.

There was a great virtue that families also trained in their children since babyhood. It was the virtue of detachment. Those who were able to learn detachment were considered mature. Attachment to material things was considered a hindrance on the road of perfection. I saw many times people giving to their friends their beloved horse, donkey, or toys that they had made. Generosity was the sign of spiritual royalty.

In advanced esoteric groups, detachment was exercised on emotional and mental levels. Students were told that everything they have or will have does not really belong to them but that they are custodians and caretakers, who must use things economically, constructively, and in a goal-fitting way.

The real school was the life with all its relationships, and there was a saying, "For those who are ready to learn, life becomes their wise Teacher."

In the olden communities, people were very direct with their children about the phenomenon of death. I remember my first lesson concerning it. My little lamb was in an accident and died. I went straight to my Father and said, "What has happened to my lamb?"

My Father sat down and took my hands in his and said, "You are asking about a great mystery, but I know you will understand it when I explain it to you. All forms," he continued, "are built of two factors, life and matter. Life grows, feels, thinks, creates; matter gives form to our life, feelings, thoughts, and creations. That is the duty of matter. When matter cannot do its duties, it disintegrates in various ways, and the life departs.

"Each human being is a life; when the body dies the life goes and forms another body and comes again into being, into matter. It is like when one goes to school and comes home, and then goes back to school again.

"Your lamb is not dead, but its body has died. The life of the lamb will come back, and you will have a new lamb."

"But, Father, isn't it painful to die?"

"It seems so for one second. But the life enjoys being out of the matter, as when we sleep and leave our body and it is not painful. When I die or when Mother dies, or anyone dies, we enter into greater life and then come back to learn more. We become happier if in our past life we were living a life of beauty. Now that you know all about this, let us go and bury the lamb."

Daddy carried the lamb toward an almond tree and dug a big hole under it and then buried the lamb. After he was done, he said, "In spring, the body of your lamb will give power to our tree and beauty to its flowers."

I remember from then on that that tree was very special for me.

Chapter Eleven

Religion and the Child

It is very interesting to note that people in these Asian communities never encouraged their children to get involved in religious practices. They thought that before choosing a religion the child must have a mind trained to analyze, discriminate, and choose by his or her own free will in order not to fall into devotional traps..

The choice of church was made only by mature people between the ages of 30 and 40. Children were not advised to attend so-called Sunday school or Bible classes. They were encouraged to read about heroes, history, and myths, to study the sciences, and to engage in sports.

The people of the communities used to think that religious doctrines and Bible study would precondition the child's mind to such a degree that he or she would not be able to free himself from the limitations of the doctrines, dogmas, and traditional influences and thus would not try to approach life through his independent logic and reasoning.

When a child became interested in religious ideas, they used to give him broad outlines. On one occasion when I asked one of my Teachers about Christ, he said, "All that I can tell you about Him is that He lived a life of beauty, goodness, truth, and simplicity. And as you live such a life you will not need to know what other people say about Him because your soul will be in contact with Him."

This small conversation saved my life. After that, I looked at Christ's Teaching as a living experience rather than a dogma, doctrine, or theology, which all seemed to me a waste of time.

When I was 14 years old, I went to a church with my Father. I had a secret wish in my heart to meet Christ. The ceremonies, the singing, the rituals were very impressive, and when it was over my Father introduced me to the Bishop who said, "I am glad to see you here."

Thank you," I said.

"Did you enjoy the hymns?" he asked.

"Yes, I did," I replied, "but . . . ."

"But what?" he asked.

After a long hesitation I turned to my Father and said in a whisper, "But where is Christ?"

My Father looked to the Bishop and expected him to answer me, but the Bishop smiled and said, "We are told by many as to where He is, but I honestly do not know."

"Too bad," I said, and walked away with wet eyes. I was hurt for days and I felt depressed because I knew my Father also had no answer.

I did not repeat my question to anyone else; I felt that to find the answer to my question was only possible in living a life of beauty, goodness, truth, and simplicity.

At that time some religious meetings were going on at our home, but my Father did not invite me and I did not feel interested in them.

One day my sister, who used to attend the meetings, said that I would enjoy being a part of the meetings. I asked her what they did at these meetings, and she replied that they prayed, meditated, and talked. I replied, "I don't want it."

"Why," she asked.

"It seems to me that it is useless."

"But," she said, "you must know what will happen when you die."

"I don't care. I am looking only for someone who knows where He is."

"Who?" she asked.

"Christ," I answered.

"Are you crazy?"

"No, I am not. Unless I meet Him, there is no one that can teach me the things I want to know."

"Father knows lots."

"He knows . . . maybe . . . but where is Christ?"

She hugged me, and I felt her tears dropping on my head — then kissing me she said, "One day we will meet Him."

A few days later I felt so badly because there was again a meeting, but my sister chose instead to play ball with me in the garden. From that day on, almost every night, instead of saying good night we used to hug each other and whisper our secret words to each other. "One day we will meet Him."

On one occasion I asked my Father about the Bible, if it is good to study it. He said he had read it from the first to the last page, seven times.

"What is your impression, Father?" I asked.

"I would not read it any more even if I had a chance," he replied.

"But I thought you were teaching the Bible in the meetings at our home."

"No, not at all."

"Really?" I asked. "Then what are you teaching?"

"It is not the time to tell you the details. You need to be mature enough before you may enter, and you may not enjoy it."

"Is it a secret?" I asked.

"No, it is not."

"Is it about any religion?"

"No, it is not."

"Then what is it?"

"It is a technique by which one can develop and come in contact with deeper realities."

"What, for example?"
"Inner and deeper realities."
"Does it really help?" I asked.
"Yes, it does."
"Then why can't I come?"
"I did not say you cannot come, but I said you may not enjoy it."
"Perhaps I will."
"Then when you are mature enough, I will consider inviting you."

Years passed, and I wandered through many schools to find the answer to my search: where and how I could meet Him. Books, priests, bishops did not interest me. It seemed to me that they did not know what they were talking about. I developed some kind of sensitivity, for when priests or bishops used to talk about Him, I was able to detect in their eyes that they were just talking and that they knew that their talk was just emotion, logic, but not experience. I was looking for someone who was in contact with Christ.

I remember the day I asked my Sufi Teacher whether he knew anyone who knew how to come in contact with Christ. He looked at me with a cold expression and gave a bad slap to my face and said, "Do not dare to ask it again."

I walked away, and from 10-15 feet I asked, "Why not?"

"Come here, and I will tell you why not."

"You will hit me again."

"I will not."

So I went close to him and sat near his knees.

He looked at me for awhile and said, "It has now been 70 years. I was looking for Him from mountain to mountain, and only a few days ago I met Him."

I jumped up and threw my arms around his neck and said with tears in my eyes, "Did you really meet Him?"

"I will talk to you later."

"When will it be possible for me to meet Him?

"When many lines meet," and he suddenly got up and walked away.

I could not sleep all the night. I was afraid to go after him, but I wanted to know more about his experience.

The next morning I went to his room. The door was open, and inside it was totally empty. He was gone.

"When many lines meet."

Real religion is a communication between you and the highest you can reach. Such communication can be possible without an organized religion. Whenever we teach beauty and truth and express goodness through our sacrificial service, we contact the Highest.

Unfortunately, the religious movements of today are brain-washing processes consisting of social gatherings, politics, business, and good times. Children must not be led by organized religions but by the ideals, ideas, and visions of the religions.

It is not good to lead children into religious practices that would mold their attitude to life, but we can give them higher principles to live by without religion. We can bring the beauty revealed by great Saviors without channeling it through an organized religion. An organized religion is separative and cannot create superior beings.

It is not good to lead children into religious conflict. Give them the essence of the religions without the spirit of separatism and pride, and teach them virtues and higher principles to live by. We can bring the beauty revealed by great Saviors without instilling antagonistic attitudes in the children.

Our religious teaching prevents children from contacting new ideas, for religions try to evaluate everything through their own belief and thus miss the new revelation. For many, many ages the children have gone through religious experiences, and most of them are ready for new visions that are more inclusive and human than what they had before. The children are sometimes different seeds from different realms, and we force them to bloom as the flower we want them to be. This is the greatest catastrophe, for you are preventing that child from bringing out his own beauty and thus fulfilling his own destiny. It is wise never to give them religious or nationalistic lectures or practices. Try to help them discipline their bodies, emotions, and minds, and then allow them to have their own responses to the Almighty Life. Any imposed Teaching is a step backward on the path of evolution.

We can show religion as a relationship between man and God, between the subjective and objective world, between the past and the whole. But in teaching it we must also find out why the religions failed to create an ideal humanity, and where they failed, and how much must be replaced of that which is obsolete until we come to the conclusion that "new wine needs new bottles," as Christ said.

Many religious people will not agree with this concept, but whether they agree or not, the New Religion, the Nature of which is synthesis, is already in the process of formation. It will take time to be a strong influence in the life of humanity, but it will be known through those who already have overcome their separativeness.

Many people ask if a young child should be taught meditation. In the early years of the child's life it is better to teach him how to observe; how to control his movements and actions and tongue; how to walk, to sit, to converse; and later how to concentrate, how to choose, and how to discriminate.

Children should first learn to discipline their bodies through dances, movements, hiking, swimming, and various other sports. Then they must discipline their emotional Nature through art, beauty, and creativity. Conditions should be created in which they care for each other, work for each other. Many games can be created to cultivate their attention, observation, concentration, and discrimination.

At a more advanced age, say 15 to 18, they can be taught how to observe their actions, emotions, and speech and to try to find the motives or sources of their actions.

On the whole, they must learn to use their threefold mechanism in such a way that this mechanism eventually helps them to attain their future plans and labors. This will continue until they are 18 to 21 years of age. Meditation can then be presented to them as the art of clear thinking for the highest good of humanity and as the best way to be creative. No meditation was done until they attained that age or had completed their second year of college or had been graduated from high school for two years. Just as one does not suggest that a girl try pregnancy before her maturity, so to make a young one meditate will have a detrimental effect on his or her future growth.

Meditation puts a heavy pressure on a child's nervous system and prepares the ground for failure in future activities. I would even say that a physically mature person must not meditate if his mind is that of a teenager. Meditation, in such cases, opens the inflow of Intuition and makes him a useless human being, or burns the fuses of his mind and makes him a burden on society.

When the brain and the mind of the child is kept healthy through age 21, that child can then load his mind with heavy studies and great creative works without any negative physical reaction. The foundation must be ready in order to build the structure of the future.

Chapter Twelve

Torchbearers

It is not necessary for a woman to have a child to be or feel as a Mother. *Motherhood is not a biological function. Motherhood is a psychological, spiritual function.* Motherhood is the power to present right conditions to make virtues grow, to cause great works to be accomplished, to make creativity bloom, and to make the race of man survive in progressive unfoldment and beauty.

In the heart of each woman, one can see a Mother. She may be a woman who gave birth to a mighty movement or inspired great men to perform heroic deeds; or she herself performed heroic acts or conceived visions for the advancement of all humanity; or she became a Mother of art and beauty.

One of the supreme duties of a woman is to be an ideal Mother, but when the children have grown to need less care from the Mother, the Mother must step into the world of politics, education, communication, arts, sciences, religion, and economics. She can bring great beauty, wisdom, and experience into these fields, or she can continue her studies along specialized lines.

I have been asked many times about the real role of the woman in world leadership. To answer this question I must build a few bridges. First, most women are anchored in their emotional vehicles. This gives the woman an advantage over man and makes her sensitive to the environment, to the people and their conditions. Her physical changes translate themselves into various emotions. She speaks a language of emotions no matter what words she uses. She speaks the same language a man speaks, but it has emotional meaning for her; it is more direct, more involved with the person. The language man speaks is translated by her into emotional meaning.

Man mostly speaks a physical language, or if he is educated, he speaks a mental language and translates the speech of the woman either into physical or mental language.

Thus, there is a gap between man and woman, but this gap is less for the woman because emotions are *inclusive,* whereas body or thoughts are *exclusive.* Body or thoughts act and think mostly for their own. Emotions are communions, sharing; thoughts are observations, analysis.

The most important labor for a woman is to raise her focus of consciousness from her emotional nature to her intuitional nature without creating a gap between them.

The emotional world of a woman is full of attachments when she develops her mind at the expense of her Intuition. These attachments make her translate the world around her through her own feelings and thoughts. She projects her feeling on all phenomena around her. This makes her self-centered, demanding, self-conscious, and even "rejectful," of others. She senses the viewpoints of others and understands them but rejects the persons.

If she succeeds in raising her focus of consciousness from the emotional to the Intuitional Plane, the attachments break, and a spirit of inclusiveness and universalism dawns in her consciousness. This is the natural path for a woman. She gives out all that she collected, all that she was serving to make her feel separate. Now in the process of giving things, she feels inclusive and universal.

Intuition is higher than the mind. Intuition is one million times faster than the mind. Man must raise himself from a mental focus to an atmic focus to transcend woman. This is very difficult to do. Only those who raise their consciousness from the mental plane to the Atmic via the Buddhic Plane, demonstrate the mastery of life. But this does not mean that woman cannot transcend herself. The next less resisting path for her is to raise her awareness from the Buddhic Plane to the Monadic via the Atmic Plane. This is really a great labor; whoever can do it is called in the East, a Tara, a woman Master, or a great Mother.

The Mother of Jesus was one of these great women who actually led the disciples into action and organized the first evangelical movement to spread the ideas of her Son.

The world leadership is going to go into the hands of those women who raise themselves from the astral to the Buddhic Plane. Signs show that women are more successful in raising their consciousness to the Buddhic Plane than men are in raising their consciousness from the mind to the Atmic Plane.

The mental plane is sometimes called "the slayer of the Real." Man is caught in a world of unreality that, for him, is the world of reality.

A young woman was talking with her scientist husband and saying, "I do not need all your theories, all your logic and politics. Just give me one minute of love. A kiss is more real than all that you think you know." This is a typical reaction from a woman, and it is based on an intuitive foundation.

Another time I heard a girl talking to her "wise" boyfriend, "Honey, please forget about the problems of the world and love me. No problem can be solved without love, and you must know what love is before you solve your problems." Of course this sounds selfish, even manipulative, but woman knows the concept is true. It has a manipulative coloring, but it is fundamentally intuitive, if understood correctly.

Because of their advantage of being more intuitive than mental, women control the actions of man behind the scenes, but mostly for their own emotional ends. *The times are changing now; women are now able to develop their minds and tap the intuitional world more than at any time of human history.* If they press on, they will lead humanity toward sanity, universalism, true peace, and understanding. All these are the gifts of the new Aquarian Age.

When a woman is stuck in her emotional attachments and does not have intuitive flashes, she becomes a victim of man. She is not only exploited but also exploits. Millions of women are manipulated by man, who uses his lower mind to misuse women for his own advantage. If a woman is stuck in her emotional nature, she has a strong tendency to depend on the man who has mind.

When the woman develops her mind, she has a tendency to take revenge on the man in many forms. Her liberation is not through her mind but through her Intuition. An intuitive woman is highly spiritual, progressive, free, and inclusive.

An emotional woman is the slave of her attachments. She is religious, but she is fanatic and separative. She leaves religions when she develops her mind, and she becomes spiritual when she becomes active in the intuitional light.

Man attacks the emotions of woman to conquer her. Woman attacks the instincts, urges, and drives of the physical nature of man to enslave him.

An intuitive woman is not caught in these games. She has a great task. Her task is to save her child and to make him grow healthy and beautiful. *Her child is humanity.* Her glory is the *culture* of her child.

An emotional woman wants to possess. Because she has occasional flashes of Intuition, especially when she suffers, she knows that her possessions do not belong to her, but she pretends that she owns them totally only to attract attention. Once she gets what she wants, she is ready to resign from all her possessions.

An intuitive woman does not like to possess because possessions limit her freedom.

An intuitive woman stands for freedom. Her freedom is an ability not to be enslaved by physical urges and drives, emotional hang-ups, or mental rationalizations but to be, instead, in a position that helps everyone to grow into freedom and creative expressions.

Once a woman said to another woman: "You are a great artist, but you are an emotional artist."

"Why do you think so?" the other replied.

"Because you make your husband your puppet or your servant. If you advance in your creativity, you will help him to liberate himself from you."

"But then I will lose him, and you will take him over!"

"If I take him over, you will have him back as a liberated human being!"

An intuitive woman hates to see man as a slave not only to other women but also to his own nature.

An advanced man who is heading toward atmic levels has a similar way of looking at a woman. A woman limited by her body, sex, possessions, and emotional hang-ups repels him, but he challenges her by his achievements and beauty. Thus he creates a great urge in her to transcend her level and get closer to him.

Some women unfold and bloom in the presence of a man who is in the light of the Atmic Plane.

Thus man and woman act as bridge and traveler alternately.

Women not only have a unique role to play with their family but also a unique responsibility to

1. protect life
2. protect the right development of life
3. evoke the highest latent in man
4. protect beauty
5. protect peace and harmony
6. protect the age-long fruits of the labor of humanity
7. protect the Teaching from degeneration
8. encourage the best in all fields
9. strive toward the future
10. learn and teach the laws of sacrifice and service
11. produce the highest survival techniques
12. inspire creativity in all fields
13. reveal the future possibilities of life after death

It is good that we celebrate Mother's Day, for it is a day during which Mothers must remind themselves of their sacred responsibilities toward life. It should be a day of true self-recollection, contemplation, and striving through which they can touch the flame within themselves and radiate it out to the needy world.

In the Agni Yoga literature we read:

. . . Truly the women must sacredly guard the chalice entrusted to them: the moving of con-

sciousness and the saving of the world. The epoch of Maitreya is the epoch of woman.[1]

It is very beautiful to see women fighting for women's rights, but it would be even greater if women would form a new group, a new organization that would reveal to humanity the responsibilities of women and fight to restore those conditions in which women would be able to perform their responsibilities.

Let us take the *first* responsibility of a woman or a Mother, which is *to protect life.* When a woman is giving birth to a life, she is going to stay with that life and she is going to preserve that life. Such a task involves all fields: social, economic, and political, wherein that woman is going to be active to protect life.

One day I received a letter from the founder of a cat foundation, and all the workers there were women. In the letter the lady said, "It is our responsibility to protect the lives of our cats." How much more effort is needed to protect the lives of millions of children throughout the world!

People have begun to work seriously against pollution, attempting to safeguard the life in the sea, the life in the air, the life in the forest, the life in the vegetable kingdom — the trees, flowers, bushes — safeguarding the life of humanity.

---

[1]. Agni Yoga Society, *Letters of Helena Roerich,* Vol. l, p. 451.

What a great thing women have to do, preserving life, protecting life. If they engage in such a task they will make tremendous strides in the world protecting life, instead of organizing dances until morning, going to bingo clubs, or sitting for many hours in front of the television set. Women can organize groups and organizations that make their voices heard all over the world declaring that life must be protected. They will affirm: "Man does not know the damage he is doing to life, and therefore we will not let him continue polluting the world. Woman is the protector of life." But if we have women who are not educated and open to such principles, to such responsibilities, then it is useless for them to bring children into our world because their children will work against life.

The *second* responsibility of a woman is *to protect the right development of life.* You have brought a beautiful baby into a world with nice trees, fish in the sea, beautiful birds in the air. Are you creating the conditions that can sustain the life of these life-forms? For example, in your schools or in your television programs, are you working for life? I received a letter that said: "We are against violence in the movies." That is good. But what are you really doing to *stop* these things? Instead we cut each other's throats or teach ways to destroy one another. What are we teaching our children so that they will support and protect life? In what way are they going to protect this life and make this life grow to become as a blooming flower, a great radioactive beauty?

Not only are women going to protect life, but they are also going to prepare the conditions in which these lives are able to grow. For example, you purchase a nice tree for your garden. It is really healthy and beautiful, but do you have a nice garden with good soil, a nice place that the sun touches? Do you have water, fertilizer, and everything needed so that the life of the tree will be sustained and continued?

This is why, when we are talking about Mothers, we are talking about responsibility. If the child is good, if he is creative, it is because his Mother kept her eye on him, not in a way that she was obsessing or possessing him, but in a way that she was inspiring and leading him into creative directions in his early years.

The *third* responsibility of a woman is *to evoke the highest latent in man*. The responsibility of the woman does not end only with her child. If she has a husband, if she has a man around her, what is she going to do? She is going to evoke or bring out the best in that man year after year. Woman can do it. I have seen it happen in many cases. Because of a woman, a man is blooming; because of a woman, a hospital was different; because of a woman, a clinic was different, a group was different.

Woman has a certain magical, mysterious way in which she evokes the best in a man. Woman is more advanced physiologically and spiritually than man, but the best the woman can bring out of the man is the best the woman has in her. She is just like a magnet. When she touches a man, when she talks to a man, when she smiles at a man, that man feels that he is getting more sublimated, more transformed because of her contact.

When we speak of contact, we are not speaking of "technique." For example, one day I met a teacher who was teaching the girls how to be "magnetic," and she was saying, "Walk like this, look like this, and fix your hair this way." She was really technically teaching them. Then I asked her, "Have you had any results?" "Curiously enough," she said, "there were results but they did not last." This is what I wanted to know. Why isn't it lasting? — Because it is artificial, a technique.

A woman must have greatness in her to bring greatness out of others. Woman must build that greatness, build that beauty, build that creative mechanism within herself so that her creative magnetism pulls the beauty out of man. If a man has the magic hand of a woman, the magic love of a woman, he will be transformed. Many, many medical expenses can be spared, many legal expenses can be stopped if the man has an understanding, compassionate, loving woman who is highly educated and highly transformed in her inner being.

The *fourth* responsibility of the woman is *to protect beauty.* Woman stands for beauty. A woman's psychology is for beauty. Woman is instinctively drawn towards beauty. For example, I was watching two little children, a boy and a girl seven and eight years old. The little girl was caring for her hair, putting on her mommy's beautiful dresses and jewelry, and trying to walk in a certain way. The boy wasn't. He wanted to play, build something, or fight; he had different motivations.

To create a child means to unify and synthesize many principles and laws in such a way that they become a body and a soul. This phenomenon appears easy. The man and woman marry and the baby comes. But it is not easy. Millions of secret and mysterious principles are working to bring a child into manifestation.

The woman stands for the expression of the Creative Principle of the Universe, and that Creative Principle stands only for the expression of beauty. The birth-giving process is an artistic procedure to manifest a beauty. Beauty is the manifestation of the harmony of the Almighty Power. When she is manifesting beauty, she is assisting the Creative Principle to manifest Itself. This Principle is manifested through her creative actions, thoughts, and emotions. She is giving birth to the great Creative Principle hidden within her.

One of the greatest responsibilities of a woman is to preserve beauty, to sustain beauty: the beauty of her environment, the beauty of her garden, the beauty of her house, the beauty of the colors in her home, the beauty in how her children are dressed, the beauty of human relationships, the beauty of the Wisdom of the Ages, the beauty of human thought, the beauty created by human labor, the beauty of the heart.

One day a Mother took her young son on a picnic. During their picnic the boy saw a pair of shoes that had been left under a tree, and he asked, "Mommy, do you know whose shoes those are?" The Mother pointed to where some children were playing and she said, "Yes, the big boy put them there a little while ago." "Oh," he said, "can I take his shoes and hide them somewhere, and when he comes to get them he won't be able to find them?" "Yes, you can do that," said the Mother, "but what could we do that would be nicer than that? What if we take one dollar from my purse and put it in his shoe and then hide, and when the boy comes we will see what will happen."

They hid behind a tree and after a while the boy came for his shoes. As he was putting them on, he felt that there was something inside one of them, and he reached in and found the dollar. "Ahhh!," he cried, "there is a dollar in my shoe! Look!" All his friends gathered around him, jumping and clapping their hands.

The little boy who was hiding with his Mother was very happy. He wanted to jump out from behind the tree and go hug the boy, but his Mother said, "Sometimes it is better not to reveal yourself when you make people happy."

There is a great beauty in inspiring our children, in showing them ways and means totally different from those impressed upon their minds by certain television shows, movies, or radio. The things that are impressed on the mind of a child stick there, and the child automatically, mechanically acts from these impressions. Mothers can erase these images by evoking beauty from the child through her love. The Mother is the guardian of beauty.

In 1938 Nicholas Roerich, a world renowned artist and philosopher, wrote an open letter to the nations of the world. He said, "Let us protect the beauties of the world from the destruction of the bombs. Let us protect our cathedrals, our museums, the creative flowers of human labor." Many people responded to the call, and the majority were women. Because of the sacrificial labor of these women, many objects of human creativity were protected in Europe and other places at the time of the war.

Woman will stand for the protection of beauty. Any time a woman sees that people are trying to destroy beauty, she has the right to inspire them to stop doing so by affirming, "The beauty of our lakes must stay; the beauty of our mountains must be kept; the beauty of our children must be protected." If women stand for beauty, no one will stand against them. Women have power: they have physical power, emotional power, mental power, spiritual power. Women have the power to evoke greater abilities and talents from their children and husbands. This is how they gain their leadership. Real leadership is the process of bringing the best out of humanity. Woman is already engaged in this great labor. A great Sage says that our solar system is a feminine solar system, and whether we like it or not, increasingly in the coming ages, woman is going to lead and rule the world.

The *fifth* responsibility of the woman is *to protect peace and harmony.* If anybody has the right to do this, it is the right of woman. I remember in the Middle East there was a disagreement between two clans, and both sides were preparing for bloodshed. Seeing the accumulating danger, the women from both sides met and decided to warn their men against such an action. Before it was too late, all the women of both parties were mobilized in such a way that they stopped any action toward bloodshed.

I heard the women saying to their husbands and sons and brothers, "If you go to war, that is the end of you. Our children's lives are more important than that for which you are fighting." I remember a very influential man saying, "Why to fight if we will lose our Mothers' and our wives' love?"

Do you see the power that the woman has?

We need right human relations in the world. Why? — Because if there are not right human relations in the world, if there is no peace in the world, the children that you raise will be ground under the wheels of the tanks or evaporated in the flames of the bombs. Your child whom you are raising is so beautiful, and everyday you are hugging and kissing him and looking toward his future. That child goes with a machine gun and kills another child, and then they kill him, and a big tank comes and grinds and mixes their bones and flesh with the earth. Is that why you are having a child? Why are you not standing for the children then? Politicians have many, many ways to convince you to let your child go to war — but the women of the earth must not let the children go if they think that it is not advantageous for the culture and civilization of the world. Put this in your mind and think about it: any two boys fighting against each other prove their bankruptcy of logic and intelligence; when they initiate violence, they prove they are not human beings but beasts. It is far less expensive to reach the women of the world and awaken them to protect peace and right human relations than to waste billions and billions of dollars as well as the resources of the earth to promote wars.

Woman is going to teach from the beginning, "My son, don't beat him. Understand him. Find ways and means to release the beauty in him; do not beat and kill him." If our children are raised in this way, they will not turn out to be the commanders and politicians who inspire us to fight.

I went to a Mother's Day party, and a man there gave a toast and said, "Our women are so beautiful. They cook for us, they give us all the sensations we need, and we must give them flowers." And the party ended like that. That is not the way to celebrate Mother's Day. The way to celebrate Mother's Day is to remind women, as well as men, that women have very deep and precious responsibilities. It will not be a worthy celebration if the women are not reminded of the greatest treasures they have within themselves and the greatest power they can exercise for the betterment of life.

If you have a physically, emotionally, mentally, and spiritually healthy woman, that woman instinctively does not stand for any separate nation. She loves her nation but all other nations as well and often thinks, "Woman must establish peace and right human relations for she stands for life." It is generally woman who thinks universally and cosmically.

It is so interesting that the first group in service for Christ was established by the Mother Mary. This is not emphasized in our New Testament because the orientation was masculine at that time. In that day and age they were in a glamor that man was everything and woman must be suppressed. Mother Mary called all of the disciples and followers of Christ around her at the time of Pentecost, and she said, "Let us establish the first group of service and inspiration to the Great Lord." And the Holy Spirit came, like tongues of flames, and the Ministry of Light was begun.

The *sixth* responsibility of woman is *to protect the agelong fruits of the labor of humanity.* This is the foundation of the law of economy. Women have a natural tendency to save. They do not want to destroy any form that cannot be replaced by a better one. My Grandmother kept dresses and uniforms that were two and three hundred years old, precious handiworks, watches, rings, and pens of great Grandfathers, and great Grandmothers. She had a room like a museum, which gave great cultural joy to many people.

The Mothers must also protect the great cultural and historic monuments in all countries and in all nations from vandalism. All those objects that radiate the labor of ages, the labor of heart and genius must be protected for the spiritual enjoyment and education of future generations.

The *seventh* responsibility of woman is *to protect the Teaching from degeneration.* What is the Teaching? The Teaching is nothing else but all the wisdom that builds the foundation of survival and the progression of all toward Infinity.

We are not referring to any certain religion or system of philosophy, but to the *essence* of all religions, all philosophies upon which rests the foundation of our survival and creativity. The Teaching can be summarized as goodness, beauty, righteousness, truth, simplicity, gratitude, harmlessness, daring, courage, forgiveness, the possibility of progressing toward Infinity, continuity of consciousness, the unity of life, sacrificial service, and joy.

There are many, many distortions in the presentation of religious teachings. In ancient Teachings, the religions were not exactly as we have been told they were. Real religion is founded on the following four principles:

>Justice
>Compassion
>Freedom
>Beauty

No matter in what different ways religions explain and interpret these four principles, the foundation remains the same. If a religion is distorted and turned into revenge or materialism, into separativeness, into the worship of pleasures and hatreds, then that religion is distorted, that philosophy is distorted, that teaching is distorted.

How can a woman safeguard the Teaching? The first thing a woman must do is to touch her own Intuition. This is a very important point. She is not going to learn the Teaching only from books. She is going to learn the Teaching by touching the innermost essence of her nature. Women can do it because they are, to a great degree, intuitively oriented. Some women can understand the Teaching without reading it at all. Some women can understand a man without talking with him. They can sense what he is. Intuitively women can see the essence of things. Women must touch this source of wisdom within themselves, the magnet within themselves, the real compassion within themselves, so that they always see the right path. Once they have made a contact within themselves, if any of the Teaching is distorted in their home, in their children, in their husband, in their society, they can stand fast, point it out, and protect the Teaching. It is the woman, the Mother, the wife who warns against any degenerative conduct or ugly behavior.

For example, I was visiting a home where the man was beating his son and yelling at him. "Why were you lying to your friends?" Then the Mother came in and said to her husband, "Think how many times you lie. You cannot talk about justice or truth if you are lying all day in your business and with your family. Why are you beating this child?" A woman can help a man stay in order because of her love. She wants to sacrifice and dedicate herself for love, for justice, for the protection of the Teaching.

Woman must forge the new life and create the new civilization, a new way of living, a new life of international relationships, a new life in society.

To do these things, woman must really be "together." How is she going to be "together?" A very simple beginning for a woman is the life of meditation — meditation and contemplation.

Intuitive contact with great ideas and great visions is easier for women than for men. They can sense the prototypes of things to come; they can really see the blueprints beyond the thoughtforms. And in seeing or sensing them, they are going to bring that beauty and plan to the earth and manifest it in their daily relationships. In order to build a new civilization, women must *know* that through their efforts a new world is going to come into existence.

How can they accomplish this? —By saving their energies: physically, emotionally, and mentally. —By saving their money. —By saving even their whole lives in order to apply their lives to a great cause. And what is that great cause? —A new civilization, a new culture. If most of the women in the world were to stand for a great vision, what a power they would present for the correction of the distortions in many areas of life.

Perhaps more important is the fact that women can influence their husbands. That is fundamental. A woman can influence her husband, her brothers, her uncles, her cousins, her family; she can influence the government; she can influence armies; she can influence any facet of Nature that is controlled by man. Actually, the primary controller is the woman, the Mother. If the Mother is able to control but is not doing it, then it means that the Mother is failing in her great responsibility.

A woman can really change a man. We find that this is so through our practical experiences.

There was a boy who was following a really destructive way of life. Then he met a girl who was so beautiful, so idealistic, so sensitive, that in a few months time that boy really changed. He had been smoking, drinking, doing many destructive things, but every time he did these things, she smiled and said, "You are bigger than that; you are more beautiful than that." The boy gradually paid more attention to what she said and slowly left his habits behind and became her beautiful husband.

Woman has a great charm that influences people and causes great psychological changes in them through her love, inspiration, and admiration, and, curiously enough, through her expectation. Expectation is an act of evocation.

Women must be reminded, especially on Mother's Day, that they have a great responsibility to face in rebuilding the world. That is why the modern woman is not going to just sit in the house. When her duties are finished, she will face great responsibilities in politics, education, science, religion, economy. In all social relationships women are going to take the reins in their hands.

Actually, in the Teaching we are told that the Epoch of Maitreya is the Epoch of Woman, that the reappearance of the Christ, the era of Christ, the era of human brotherhood, the era of one humanity is the era of womanhood. It is the era of the Mother.

Does that seem very strange? If it is really to be so, then woman is going to have to work very hard on herself. Physically, emotionally, mentally, spiritually, socially, she must come together to such a degree that she radiates a great vision with enough potency, enough power that humanity grasps and follows that path of liberation.

A great Sage says that Buddha held woman in the greatest esteem and stated that the woman, as well as the man, can achieve the highest degree of spiritual enlightenment. There are many great women in the history of humanity who have lighted the way toward love, sacrifice, knowledge, and true leadership.

As it has been stated before, gradually it will be women who are going to take the role of leadership into their hands. The woman is going to rule. But when we say she is going to "rule," we immediately mistranslate that word through our associative thinking. "Rule" means, here, to present the vision in such a way that the efforts and labors of people are magnetically oriented toward that vision. Such a way of ruling creates incentives toward a greater goal. This is what is meant by ruling.

Actually women have been inspirers in all ages, and they will increasingly inspire more and more until all departments of human endeavor are oriented towards a life based on the Teaching. This does not belittle man. Man's joy and success is to manifest the vision and bring it into full actualization.

The concept of the *Mother of the World,* the Creative Feminine Principle, is a supreme concept.

Chapter Twelve — Torchbearers

If only our Mothers, sisters, wives, and daughters would identify themselves with that concept and really think as if they were the Mother of the World, the Creative Feminine Principle.

In esoteric philosophy, women are identified with the principle of the Holy Spirit, Which inspires, gives vision, and works for all. Esoterically, this inspiration reactivates all treasures in the Chalice, reconditions the records of the permanent atoms, and directs the life of the child and the man toward improvement.

Some people think that because we have the conditioning factors in our permanent atoms and genes, we cannot change anything.[2] This is wrong. Actually the whole foundation of education is based on the fact that we can recondition and improve things. If, for example, evil and good are half and half in me, I can be both. But if I meet a woman, or a Mother, or a wife who will inspire me toward good, my goodness then will increase and my evil tendencies will decrease. But if the woman I meet is of low order, then I have little chance to escape my evil tendencies.

I was in Germany, and one night I saw that there was an American film playing in a nearby theater. I said, "Good, it is an American film; let

---

[2.] See *The Science of Becoming Oneself*, Ch. 12, for more information concerning the "permanent atoms."

me go see it." I paid for my ticket and went in and the film started. A lady came on the screen as an embodiment of fear and crime and began to scream, "My jewels! They stole them. Kill them. Destroy them." It was so emotional, so criminal. I left the theater with sorrow in my heart, thinking, "We, a leading nation of the world, are exporting films of crime and violence to other countries."

Nations must export ideas of beauty, ideas of right human relations, ideas of world justice and freedom through films, magazines, and papers. If they create and export films that will show the dignity of women and the responsibilities of women and men, they can spread a new education all over the world. It is the duty of women to inspire such an idea in all those who are involved with the media.

If women everywhere educate humanity in high ideals, this will bring about material as well as spiritual benefit. It will greatly cut all our expenditures if all countries are in harmony with each other. Women can do a great deal in spreading to other countries the highest ideals and beauties that the human spirit possesses.

The *eighth* responsibility is *to encourage the best in all fields*. Woman can do this. She says, "I love that book, that movement, that company, that president, that music because it helps our unity, our

Chapter Twelve   *Torchbearers 257*

understanding; it leads to sharing, nobility of spirit." When woman admires, man follows because he wants to be admired by woman. It is an instinct in him. Woman knows how to do this without criticism and without hurting anyone. She says, for example, "I enjoyed all of it but that certain point was special." And if she emphasizes that point and draws the attention of the man to the best, then that man will try to do the best. But, as has been said, this ability rests on her education and intuitive perceptions.

The *ninth* responsibility is to *strive toward the future*. "My son, my love, whatever you say, whatever you do is good for today, for the present moment. But is it good for the future, for the coming ages in which a greater light will shine and there will be a greater unity and greater revelations?" Isn't such a woman beautiful? When she says, for example, "I know you failed many times, but you can do it if you try again. You are not going to give up; others did it, so you do it. The future is just waiting for you. I will admire you again; stand up. Do not give up. We can do it together. Tomorrow will be the day of our victory over our weaknesses." Or she may say, "I do not care how much money you make by way of lies and robbery. I am worrying about our future, about the future of our children, about their karmic burdens. Let us be poor but honest. Let us have a small house but peaceful minds. It is much better for our future. The present moment is very short, but the future is endless. Let us work for the future." Imagine such a woman.

The *tenth* responsibility of a woman is *to learn and to teach the laws of sacrifice and service.* The Mother knows that the greatest virtue of a human being is the ability to sacrifice and serve. That is what a Mother is; she has the innate drive to serve and to sacrifice for all her beloved ones, thus giving an example to them to serve and sacrifice for each other.

Imagine an organization of women who will hold this principle of service and sacrifice in front of all humanity, and through all their creative expressions, movies, articles, books, lectures, they will emphasize the need to sacrifice for each other and to serve each other. What an educational river will flow into the hearts of humanity when the women of the world respond to such a call and take global action.

To sacrifice is to give your utmost to make a group closer to their highest visions. To serve is to show the way to do it.

The *eleventh* responsibility of the woman is *to produce the highest survival techniques.* Peace, cooperation, sharing, unity, and honesty constitute the five-pointed star of the new technique of survival. It is the woman in all educational fields who must emphasize these principles, for it is only through these principles that our children will have greater success and joy in life.

Who are her children? They are the children of all nations, even children of the so-called enemies of her nation. She will prove that peace brings more interest than war. Cooperation creates greater success for all. Sharing makes one enjoy his portion more. Unity makes us economize the energies of Nature and dispel all the fears and limitations of our conditioning. Honesty brings one's spiritual treasures forth into expression and establishes world-wide trust. It is the Mothers who are going to shine the light of this five-pointed star all over the world as the technique of survival in the New Age.

I know some Mothers who have lost their children in the war. Every time a young boy enters the homes of these Mothers, they cry. When a friend came to say good-bye to his dead friend's parents, the Mother embraced him for a long time and said to him with tears in her eyes, "Don't be killed like my son." There is a greater psychic affinity, oneness, sensitivity between the Mother and her children and even the children of others.

When women stand for life, no power can defeat them. In the Teaching, which is all the accumulated wisdom of the ages, it says that the greatest healing power is a woman's heart, but it is not referring to emotion or symbolism. It is referring to some kind of emanation from the heart center of the woman that heals, encourages, inspires, and enlightens. Women can use their power of heart in healing the wounds of nations, inspiring them toward greater unity and cooperation, and enlightening the leaders with the light of their hearts.

The *twelfth* responsibility of the woman is *to inspire creativity in all fields*. Woman is the guardian of all the treasures of humanity, but this does not mean that she is bound to the past. If you closely study the psychology of woman, you can see that the greatest urge in her is the urge to create and to inspire others to be creative.

The word "creative" is used here in another sense, in its higher sense. You can create a symphony, but you must be creative in your self-actualization. What is being referred to here is the creativity through which the hidden beauty, the hidden divinity within you starts to manifest in your daily relationships, in your physical, emotional, and mental activities, in your plans and motives.

Woman not only gives birth physically to her child, but she can also conceive him spiritually and give birth to his spiritual nature as well. Some women will be fearful in the face of such responsibilities, but if they delve deep down into their hearts, they will touch the heroic fire waiting there.

Woman has a very effective way of evoking the creative powers of man. Her love, her attention, her presence supply the elements that man uses to manifest his creative ideas. Man blooms and radiates under the rays of love from a woman who can inspire him with vision, courage, daring, and striving. Most of the great works of a man are done under the inspiration of a woman who is able to focus his creative energies toward the highest ideals and visions.

Not only physical creation needs male and female elements, but mental creativity and spiritual creativity also need the subtle elements of the male and female to substantiate them and to be effective in changing the level of human life.

The elders used to think that no real man must humiliate a woman because the humiliation of woman brings the downfall of the man. They also said that exploitation of woman by the man is the downfall of the man.

Pornography weakens the sexual urge and energy in man. People use pornography to satisfy their thirst for sex because of the weakness of their organs. I saw many impotent men who, because of their dead organ, were worshipping the nude pictures of women to enjoy them in their imagination and replace the need for normal sex.

When woman is exploited in the media, it reflects on the integrity of the man and lowers his value and dignity as a man. The most dignified man is one who respects the woman with full sincerity. The woman's love and inspiration makes a man transform himself and bloom.

Woman generally never exploits man unless she wants to take revenge upon him. It is the man who exploits the woman — her body, her acts, and her emotions — to make money and to have success. The elders used to think that every time a woman is misused, the man loses his main sense of support, which is the woman.

A misused and exploited woman cannot inspire, encourage, direct, and be supportive to a man.

One day I heard an older man talking to his son, saying, "My son, the success of man is mostly conditioned by the inspiration and love of the woman.

The *thirteenth* responsibility of woman is *to reveal the future possibilities of life after death.* The woman does not limit the guidance of her children just to the field of earthly life. She feels in her heart and through her own Intuition that life should not end on earth but should continue forever. Man can intellectually admit such a postulate, but the woman feels it. In giving birth to a living form, she comes in closer contact with life, and to a certain degree, she identifies with life. She comes in contact with the living entity, the unborn child who is in the process of building his body. It is impossible for her to believe that the life and the being she has contacted in her pregnancy and during the nursing period can die and vanish. Her psychic nature, her intuitive contacts give her the conviction that life will continue even after the body is dead. She has this inner conviction, even if it is clouded by materialistic pressures of many kinds.

Woman is the bridge that links the subjective and objective worlds, the world of soul and the world of body, within herself. Psychologically woman has a closer contact with the spiritual world than man due to her intuitive perception and sensitivity. That is why in Eleusiian, Zoroastrian, and Egyptian mysteries the connecting link between the subjective and the objective worlds were virgins who acted as mediators between the world of wisdom and vision and the world of everyday life and its problems.

Virgins, in the mystery temples, esoterically were those women whose focus of consciousness was totally anchored in the Intuitional Plane. They were never interested in their reproductive systems due to their sublimation in previous lives. Because of this, they were able to contact higher forces and become transmitters of great visions, ideas, and revelations. Many women in history, after having a contact with the supernatural, lifted their focus of consciousness to the Intuitional Plane and gave humanity a supreme Teaching and a great beauty, gradually ending their physical level relationship with their beloved one.

Contact with higher forces requires that the subject should use her or his forces very discriminately. That is why monasteries were established and convents were in operation for many, many centuries. Of course, the existence of monasteries and convents did not guarantee that the students or members were really heading toward total sublimation, but that was the preordained goal.

It is very rare to find real virgins who are not only withdrawn from their physical activities but also are withdrawn from the emotional and mental counterparts of sexual desire.

The responsibility of women is to direct our attention to the fact of the continuity of life and advise us to live wisely on the path of Infinity.

Psychologically, the Mother cannot accept the death of her children. *Isis* was a Mother-Goddess who emphasized this fact. She stood as a bridge between life and life after death. It is the Mother's responsibility to emphasize *life,* the continuous life, like a thread on which our short lives are as beads. To do this, woman needs to educate herself to prove to her children her innate conviction of immortality.

It is amazing to see that in all esoteric fields, the women are the majority, and not only in attendance and study but also in leadership. In the past one hundred years we have had very remarkable women in the field of esotericism who gave us a greater hope for the future. We have Helena Petrovna Blavatsky, Alice A. Bailey, Helena Roerich, and many other great ones who spoke and wrote about life after death and about the continuity of consciousness. A Mother stands for life. She instinctively knows that there is no death, and she is going to teach this fact in our modern language of science.

A Mother is a link between the Fiery World and the physical plane. In her these two worlds meet, and that is why she is aware of the Fiery World, psychic realms, and the orientation of the physical world to them.

The last, or *fourteenth*, responsibility of women is *to explain the law of love and compassion*. Mothers know more about love than anybody else in humanity. The heart of the Mother embraces the entire existence. She intuitively feels that she is one with the Creative Principle in the Universe, and in her best moments, you see her identified with that Principle in bliss, in ecstasy, in giving all that she has and is. If you do not "re-program" her, her love is for all. There is no division in her love, and her love is to light the fires of striving in all whom she meets.

The Mother feels at one with the love that makes the trees to bloom, the flowers to radiate their fragrance, the birds to sing, the rivers to flow, the oceans to roar, the sun to rise, and the stars to shine. She knows that there is no true joy, no true creativity, no true success except through love. All joy and all pain sound an echo in her heart. That is why she is the dispenser of love and compassion.

Imagine a woman being the expression of love in her home or in any place where she is found. Imagine what a stream of joy will flow there, how much healthier and brighter will be her children, how much more peaceful will be her husband, her boss, and everyone working with her. She will dispel hatred. She will spread tolerance, forgiveness, and right human relations. She will increase goodwill. She will build bridges of understanding and cooperation. She can do all these things because she knows the value of life and the value of each human being. She is naturally prepared to share her life and sacrifice it for those whom she loves.

This fourteenth responsibility, to explain the law of love and compassion, actually synthesizes all her responsibilities. A woman is equal to her heart. As the heart is to the body of a man, so the Mother is to the world. If she really recognizes this reality, she has a tremendous responsibility to be a heart, a source of compassion on earth. You can imagine if a woman really protects this right, really emphasizes compassion in her home, in her relationships with her children and husband, in her relationships to society, to the nation, to humanity, she will promote a new life in the world.

Compassion is more elevated and deeper than love, for compassion is inclusive and has no separative elements in it. Compassion is all unifying. If women really emphasized compassion in all their relationships, what great changes would evolve in the world.

When a child abuses a bird, cat, dog, or any living thing, a Mother, because of her compassion, instructs the child why he must not hurt or kill these things. She explains that every time he kills, every time he distorts, or every time he hurts and destroys, he is not behaving compassionately. If the woman extends this idea toward humanity and nations and emphasizes this relationship in our politics and religions, a great change will happen in the world because compassion is the root of understanding.

H.P. Blavatsky, a great woman of the 19th century, said, "The very nature of compassion is harmony." Whenever there is compassion, within yourself, within your family or nation or group, then there is harmony. Compassion fosters beauty, harmony, and harmlessness. The great beauty of a Mother is to teach the children the real essence of harmlessness, beauty, and harmony.

To have compassion means to have a love that is not limited to your physical or emotional sentiments, nor by partial intentions or conditions. It is limitless. It is love for the sake of the life of every atom, of every cell, of every life-form; it is all-inclusive love not only of humanity but of everything that exists. Compassion is a love that really harmonizes. If you consider love at the present stage of human understanding, it is only partial in our minds. You say, "I love my country," but actually you are telling me that there are other countries you do not love. That is not compassion. Compassion is love for all.

In India, many spiritual groups worship the *mother,* the World Mother. The World Mother is the principle of Compassion. The heart of the woman can respond to the needs of all life-forms if it is kept free of separativeness and crystallizations. The heart of the woman even senses the pulse of the life-forms of vegetable, animal, human, and superhuman forms. Because of her compassion she achieves great heights of understanding life. Through compassion she initiates herself into greater states of awareness.

Conscious women. This is what is needed in our social, economic, and political worlds. The new-age woman will teach through all the avenues of human endeavor one great subject: the value of life. She is going to find out how to change this distorted world into a family of nations in which human life is not wasted. She will make sure that right conditions prevail to insure that the coming generation will be able to create a new culture, a new civilization based on the principles of purity, beauty, and love.

The women of the world hold our destiny in their hands. Let their strength increase year after year.

As I end this writing, I am remembering a beloved friend of mine. It was during the great war, and he was dying of burns all over his body.

"Is it possible," he whispered to me, "to see my Mother?"

"Your Mother has been told, and we are waiting for her."

"I want to live until my Mother comes."

The boy's Mother came after traveling for two days. Her son was still alive, but in great pain and suffering.

His Mother was a very beautiful woman. In dignity and solemnity she entered the room and went over to her son. She put his head on her heart and said, "I am here."

"Mother, I waited for you to tell you how much I love you."

"I know...."

And he passed away. Through my tears, I was watching her. It seemed to me that she was hugging all children of the world.

In my suffering for both of them, I went over to her and put my hand on her shoulder and said, "Do not let us die anymore!" She looked at me with big tearful eyes and said, "We must not fail in the future."

This was a promise for me, and I wanted, in my own way to remind her of her great promise for coming generations.

Index

A

Abortion 14, 15
Abstinence 63
Acts, disrespectful 150
Admiration
　ecstasy of 116
　effect 116
Advice. criticism for giving 149-150
Affirmation of women 240
Alcohol and tobacco 106
Animals and
　child 130
　pregnant woman 114
Appreciation explained 152
Aquarian Age, gifts of 235
Arts and sciences, and pregnant woman 109
Ashrams, couples, related to 90
Aspiration 104
Atlantis and sex 63
Atmic Plane 234, 237
Attachments, danger of 233
Auras, fusing of 44

B

Babies, attacks on 117-118
Baby
　and
　　cleanliness 127
　　toys 130
　atmosphere for 16
　bed for 126
　how protected 128
　permission to have 94
　rhythmic care for 129-130
　room for 126
Barley water 106
Beauties, list of 244
Beauty 132
　sharing of 170
Bed, separate 128-129
Beggars 213
Birth
　father present at 112-114
　kinds of 231
　of child, two channels of 138
Blavatsky, H.P. and compassion quote 267
Boy, qualities of 20
Breast
　feeding 123, 128
　massage 106
Brotherhood, ideal of 179
Buddha's respect for woman 254
Business 21

C

Camera, pregnant woman like 114-115
Candle ceremony for married couples 51-52
Celibacy 30, 61-63
Centers, fusing of 44
Ceremony of integration 67
Chalice 255
Chaos iv
Character
　of child, building of 141
　necessity for building 162

Child
  and
    dependence on mother 185
    independence 131
    nobility 138
  attacks on integrity of 150
  development, virtues to cultivate 142
  difficulty of raising 138
  intentions for 70
  meaning of creating 243
Children
  and
    creating independence 139
    disfigured toys 143
    meditation 228
    playing in Nature toys 143-145
    promises 150-151
    punishment 142
    relation to mother 183
    responsible father 179
    self-discipline 204
    time of father 171
  beautiful 3
  beauty of 214
  covering heads 130-131
  exposed to world evil 162
  father teaching virtues 171
  fatherless 30
  helping 144-145
  how inspired 245
  living in mother 184
  need for trust in parents 151
  needs of 169
  negative conditions for 159
  new-age 206
  of
    bad influences 160-161

    New Age 162
  qualities to nurture 137
  teaching discrimination to 161
  teaching of 131, 133
  unschooled 207
  unwanted 8
  why kept busy 208
Children's deeds, how not tolerated 199
Christ's Teaching as living experience 222
Circumcision 124-125
Class, 5 year 1-2
Clowns, pictures of 114
Communication
  importance of 173
  in family 170
Community, morality of
Compassion
  as harmony 267
  teaching to children 267
Conception
  conscious 83-91
  science of 95
  timing of 94
Conscious unity 43
Cooking 11
Counseling
  couples 175
  of married couples 50-52
Couple, integration and goal, dedication to 43-44
Couples, spiritually advanced 28
Courage 75
  tested 21
Creativity
  after intercourse 45

Creativity
  def. of higher 260
  elements, male and female 261
  of father 177-178
  protection of human 245
Crime 7
  noise as cause of, 110
Crimes, finding causes of 163
Crises
  creators of 90
  souls as 90
Cross, symbol of 72
Crown, sacred 72
Culture of New Age 190
Customs and rules, observation of 135
Cycle, conflicting with 193
Cycles
  feminine and masculine 190
  synchronizing with 193

D

Dance, effects of 102
Death
  and child 218
  and life 265
Dedication to a cause 31
Destruction of family 174
Detachment, child trained in 217
Direction iv
Discipleship, living double life of 216
Discrimination 133
Divorce 7, 58
  preventing 175
Doubt 150

Drugs and children 159

E

Earth, feminine 190
Economy 12-13
Economic conditions 28
Education
  beginning of 195
  contrasted with old 203
  for Motherhood 194-197
  new-age 203
Elderly, respect for 10
Elders, role of 2-23
Embryo
  and mental, emotional nourishment 109
  effects on 115
Emotions
  effect on embryo 109
  advantages of 232
Encouragement explained 152
Engagement 37, 40
Evil and preparing children 162
Export of ideas 256

F

Families, duty to child 49
Family
  as school for soul 61
  consecrated 66
  contacts that harm 60
  creativity in 178
  destruction of 174
  four cornerstones of 165
  goals of 175
  ideal 179

Family
  meetings 59
  need for vision 174
  power of 179
  reputation of 23-25
  social level of 23
  survival of 2
Father
  and
    baby 126-127
    beautiful qualities of 180
  as
    example 176-177
    provider of right conditions 171
  creativity of 177-178
  def. of 166
  duties of 165-166
  how to respect and care for 180-181
  preparation for 167
  presence at birth 112
  progress of 167
  qualifications for 166
  reflect on 180
  responsibilities in marriage 167
  training children in virtues 171
Fatherhood, list of responsibilities 167-178
Father's Day, true celebration of 166
Feminine nature, characteristics of 193
Feminine Principle, concept of 254
Fighting as proof of bankruptcy 247

Finance and father 168-170
Financial stability, importance of 118-119
Five-pointed responsibility, course of 1-2
Flattery
  explained 152-153
  vs. encouragement 152
Folk dance festivals 102
Food 105
  and mother 105
Forgiveness, difficulty of teaching 150
Forms, beautiful 114-116
Foundation, defined 163
Friends, reputation of 60
Full Moon and sex 54
  list of potentials during 54
Funnel
  creating 84
  for incarnating life 44

G

Games and education 205
Generosity 217
Girls, education of 209
Goals of family 175
Grace, before meals, def. of 178
Grandmother, role of 128
Gratitude 74, 132
Greece, higher rules in 34
Groups
  relation to 90
  subjective 90
Guardian Angels of couple 41

H

Harmlessness, def. of 87-88
Health
  and Father 167-168
  investigations for 5-7
  mental 6
Heart
  emanation from, uses for 260
  qualities 9
  quality 26
Heroes 34-35
  and effect on mother 104
  effect on baby 104
  stories of 104
Heroism defined 104
Higher forces, contact with 264
Higher mind, marriage on 42-43
Homes, distorted, factors for 29
Homosexuality 45-47
Holy Spirit 255
Housekeeping 11
Human soul 14
Husband
  gratitude for 114
  importance of 97
Husbands, wise choice of 97
Hypnotism 107-108

I

Idea, amplification of 86-87
Ideals, high 256
Ideas, def. of 85-86
Identity, sense of 46-47
Impressions, registration in children 151
Independence
  how developed 130
  spirit of 133
Initiate doctor-priests 94
Inner Guides 41
Intercourse
  and damage to embryo 111
  as
    flame 47
    sacrifice 48
  creative energy in 45
  inner nourishment from 45
  limited 48
  limits to 48
  natural 45-47
  on higher levels 47
  positive effects of 45
  results of 46
  rewards of 48
  secrets of 44
Intuition
  cause of polarity as woman 191
  energy of 189
  from woman 189
  marriage on 42-43
  perception 26
Intuitional Plane, characteristics of 253
Investigation
  of body 3-5
  results of 4
  secrecy
    for 17
    of 4
Investigations before marriage 2-25

Isis and children 264
Isolation 100
   and mother 100

J

Joy 75-76
   as vitamin 178
   effects of 178
   from creativity 178

K

Karma and family 61
Karmic liabilities and children 140
Knowledge, heart 134

L

Law of Economy, foundation of 249
Leaders, building 162
Leadership
   by woman 246
   description of 215
   honor of 215
   of world and women 234
   qualifications for election 215
Lessons in womb, seven 195-197
Life as a school 34
Living together 62
Love
   and
      problem solving 235
      sex 49
   as flame 47
   difficulty of teaching 160
   intelligent 132
Loves, greater 49

M

Magnetic cords in marriage 57-58
Maitreya, Epoch of 253
Man
   and
      admiration 257
      atmic focus 234
      woman, bridge and traveler 237
   advanced, repelled by limitations 237
   and qualities of 168
   betterment of 168
   joy and success of 254
   most dignified, def. of 262
   right one, qualities of 18-23
   true 49-50
   characteristics of 49-50
Manliness, sense of 46
Marriage
   as
      friendship 41
      symbol of unity 41
   candidate, informing of 17
   consecration of 65
   dissolution 58
   dissolution, reasons for 58
   goal(s) of 31-32, 65-66
   higher requirements for 32
   ideal attitude of 41
   in future, permission for 32
   investigations before 2-25
   jobs and obligations in 58-59

Marriage
　journey, symbolized 66-80
　keynote of 67
　law of 32
　magnetic cords in 57-58
　main intention for 8
　partner, unfaithful 57-58
　real 41-42, 43
　service project in 43
　sharing tasks 58
　supreme duty of
　symbol, flame as 47
　wrong 3
Married couple counseling 50-52
Mary, Mother, service of 248
Masculine nature, characteristics of 193
Masturbation 124
　damage caused by 156-157
Meditation
　and consciousness 216
　def. of 86-87
　　for child 229
　effects of, 116-117
　for babies 83, 84-87
　form for Mother 120-122
Memorization, problems with 204
Memory, related to noise 110
Men, language of 232
Mental
　attitude and embryo 109
　health 103
　　and nature 103
　plane, "slayer of Real" 234
Monadic Plane 234
Monks, celibate 62

Mother
　and impression on child 184
　as
　　child's refuge 183
　　example 141
　　foundation of civilization 119
　　inspirer of heroes 140
　　protector of culture 249
　　standard 93
　　teacher 197
　gives higher births 197
　of
　　future 95
　　the World, concept of 254
　　World, worship of 268
　stands for 163
Mother's Day 194, 238
　party 248
Mother's milk, carrier of emotions 112
Mother
　disciplines for 133-134
　duty of 178-179
　grace of 186
　guidelines for 95
　how to talk to son, husband 198
　influence of 95-96
　needed 95
　new 123
　　guides for 123
　plants seeds of future 95
　quality of 93
　reasons for power 186-192
　-to-be, responsibility of 97
Motherhood
　def. of 231
　preparation for 97, 137

Motherhood
  term of 185
  training for 98
Mothers
  as foundation 18
  role of 131-132
Music
  danger of 101
  effect on mother 101
Nature
  beauty of and mother 100
  protection of by women 245
  sounds of 103
    and effect of nervous system 103

N

Negative influences 106-107
New
  Age, work of woman in 190
  cycle 120
  race, qualities of 120
News, disturbing, as shocks 108-109
Nicholas Roerich, letter to world 245
Noise
  109-111
  effects of 110

O

Objects, influences on 118
Obsession
  and possession 96
  cause of in embryo, 117
Olive oil 105-106

Organization 13
Orgasm 44
  transfer of energy in 125

P

Parents
  conduct between 150
  duty of 2
Partner
  choosing of 2-25
  qualities, projects for 175-176
Patience 75
Pentecost, events of 248-249
Permanent atoms, reconditioning of 255
Pictures, effects of 115
Plan
  creating a family 175
  Divine, def. of 85
  effects of 175
Polarities, defined 189
Polarity, characteristics of
  feminine 192
  masculine 192
Pornography 161, 261
Possession, cause of in embryo 117
Prana 45, 100
  and mother 100
Prayers, effects of 116-117
Pregnancy and guidelines 129
Pregnant woman
  and lower psychics, 117
  points for 98
Prevent crime 198
Priests 62

Principles to
   live by 227
Principles to
   teach and women 201
Problem solving 132
Proclamations, five of
Woman's Day 194-202
Property, sacredness of 213
Psychic energy 100
Psychic energy and prana 100
Purpose, def. of 192

Q

Quote:
   Agni Yoga on women 238
   Bhagavad Gita 88-89
   women and building 202

R

Rebirth, explaining to child 218
Relationships
   and pleasure 62
   changes of 62
Religion
   and education 205
   def. of 104-105
      real 226
   eliminating the obsolete parts 228
   essence of list 249
   four principles of 250
   free choice of child 221
   real 250
Religious 206
   ideas, giving outlines 222
Remarriage 58

Reputation of family 23-25
Respect
   and trust, how to create 150
   defined 180
Responsibilities
   and father 167-178
   of women 239
Responsibility course 158
Retirement, condition of self-sufficiency 216
Retreat 61
Right human relations, need for 247
Rings, symbol of 81
Ritual of marriage 66

S

Sacrifice 132-133
   defined i, 258
Sacrificial service 75
Schooling
   alternative 206-207
   forced ideas about 209
Schools, grade standard 213
Seeds, def. of 95
Self-mastery, benefits of 158
Sense of responsibility, developing in children 59
Service 132
Service
   defined 258
   project in marriage 43
Sex
   abstaining from 128
   anatomy of, how to teach 159-159
   and
      sublimation 45

Sex
  and
    woman, as advantage 186
  gift from God 63
  course on 153-154
  cyclic 44
  flame of, 46
    as protection 46
  identity and polarity 192
  life 14
  natural effects of 56
  opinion of Dervish Teacher 63
  oral 55
  oral, effects of 55-57
  positive effect of 45
  premature, damage caused by 154
  reasons for child to wait 154
  teaching children about 153-157
Sexual
  contact and saturation of force 129
  discipline 111-114
    and father 111
    effects on father 112
  energy, benefits of saving 155-157
Shakespeare 33
Shield, building 138
Sleep, proper 156
Social level of family 23
Solar system, feminine 189, 246
Solemnity 76
Son's expectation of father 177

Soul
  genius 89
  incoming 89
  requirements of 89
  symbol in literature 42-43
Souls
  great 90
  stages of development 84-85
Speech, conservation of, child trained in 217
Spirit aspect, cultivating 138-139
Spiritual
  development 227
  life, conditions for 216
  reawakenings, inspired by woman 192
Standards, raising of 206
Stars
  effect of 101
    on mother 101
Staying single 29
Stimulants, artificial 129
Story of:
  boy mastering violin/evoking greatness 33
  boy using drugs/ power of woman's influence 186-187
  boy's destructive life/inspired by girl 253
  bundle of sticks/teaching unity of family 181-182
  cowardly boy/courage and fearlessness 22
  death of lamb/teaching child about death 218-219
  doctor with no vision for family 174

drug seller/thanksgiving 199
father camping with son/ teaching bravery and caution 171-173
fearless son/relaxation with father 177
food for picnic/generosity, nobility 20-21
girl washing dishes/economy 13
girl who broke engagement/flirtation 37-40
girl's letter to cheer Torkom/woman's power to uplift 188-189
house built on rock/marriage that endures 43-44
lamb rescued from river/fearlessness and courage 22-23
leather patches/economical wife 13
man and war/ Mother's promise 269
man and woman climbing tree/assisting each other 42
man who killed enemies/confusing children 160
mayor with no diplomas/beingness of true leader 215
mother and retreating sons/ encouraging victory 139
mother and teen/irresponsibility 198
of beating son/being an example 251
old man and vitality/secrets of 157-158
relatives wasting couple's money "hungry eyes" 26-28
secretly putting money in another's shoe/making other's happy 244
son taken to Sage for lying/ father as example for son 176
Sufi Teacher who met Christ 225
teaching girls, technique of being magnetic/ lasting guidelines 242
Torkom's crime film/ exposing fear 255
Torkom's wish to meet Christ 222
TS and bear/detachment 145
woman, emotional artist/ advancing creativity 237
women not letting two armies fight/power of woman 246
Striving 133
Sublimation technique 48
Suicide 6-7
Surroundings, beauty of 114
Swords, ceremony of two 76-77
Symbol in marriage ritual 66

T

Tara 234
Teacher's life as an example 206
Teacher, new-age 206
Teachers, private 212

Teaching
    def. of 249
    how to safeguard 250
Television
    danger from radiation 101-102
    effect of 115-116
Temple of God, building of 98
Test of Turkish bath 5
Thoughts, def. of 85
Thunder, as curative 103
Tolerance 75
Torkom's grandmother 249
Toy, non-commercial 144
Toys
    greed for 143
    right meaning of 148
Transpersonal Self, contacting 54
Trust, foundation of 151-152

U

Understanding 26
Unfaithful marriage partner 57-58
Universities for motherhood 119-120
Unmarried relationship "living together" 29-30
Unwed mother 15-16

V

Value, woman's sense of 50
Virginity 125
Virgins and mystery temples 263
Virtue, greatest 258

Virtues, i
    for child, list of 141-142
    seven 73-75
    taught by father, list of 165-166
    teaching of 166
Vision
    as expectation 177
    giving spiritual, to child 174
Visitors
    and the baby 127
    character and appearance 107

W

Welfare 213
Woman
    and
        intuitive sensitivity 187-189
        ladder of evolution 191-192
        life of meditation and contemplation 251
        purpose 192
    as
        bridge 263
        creative Principle of Universe 243
        guardian of treasures 260
        teacher of understanding 247
        victim, cause of 235
    charm of 253
    degeneration of 191
Woman
    developing
        Intuition 236

Woman
  developig
    mind 236
  duties of 231
  effect of developing mind
    233
  failure of 185
  greatest image 260
  heart of i
  in
    business, two results 191-
      192
    history, work of 254
    leadership 254
    inner contacts of 252
    labor of 233
    love of, defined 265-266
    modern, greater responsibili-
      ties of 253
    new labors for 251
    preparing conditions 241
    promises of 194
    real characteristics of 198-
      199
    results of denying intuition
      191
    rights of 194
    stands for 163
    touching her essence 250
    unique responsibility of 237
Womanliness, sense of 46
Women
  and
    direction to men 184
    esoteric fields 264
    men and creative powers
      261
    spiritual birth 260-261
    standing for children 247
  universal thinking 248
  exploited, dangers of 262
  how undefeated 259-260
  language of 232
  new-age of
  powers of 246
Woman's
  Day 194
  period 52-53
    effects of 53
  sense of value 50

About the Author

Torkom Saraydarian (1917 – 1997) was born in Asia Minor. Since childhood he was trained in the Teachings of the Ageless Wisdom.

He visited monasteries, ancient temples, and mystery schools in order to find the answers to his questions about the mystery of man and the Universe.

He lived with Sufis, dervishes, Christian mystics, and masters of temple music and dance. His musical training included the violin, piano, oud, cello, and guitar. It took long years of discipline and sacrifice to absorb the Ageless Wisdom from its true sources. Meditation became a part of his daily life, and service a natural expression of his soul.

Torkom Saraydarian dedicated his entire life to the service of his fellow man. His writings and lectures and music show his total devotion to the higher principles, values, and laws that are present in all world religions and philosophies. These works represent a synthesis of the best and most beautiful in the sacred culture of the world. His works enrich the foundational thinking on which man can construct his Future.

Torkom Saraydarian wrote a large number of books, many of which have been published. All of his books will continue to be published and distributed. A few have been translated into Armenian, German, Italian, Spanish, Portuguese, Greek, Dutch, and Danish.

He left a rich legacy of writings and musical compositions for all of humanity to enjoy and benefit from for many years to come.

Visit our web site at *www.tsg-publishing.com* for more author information.

Other Books by Torkom Saraydarian

- The Ageless Wisdom
- The Aura
- Battling Dark Forces
- The Bhagavad Gita
- Breakthrough to Higher Psychism
- Buddha Sutra — A Dialogue with the Glorious One
- Challenge for Discipleship
- Christ, The Avatar of Sacrificial Love
- A Commentary on Psychic Energy
- Cosmic Shocks
- Cosmos in Man
- The Creative Fire
- Dynamics of Success
- Education as Transformation, Vol. I
- Education as Transformation, Vol. II
- The Eyes of Hierarchy—How the Masters Watch and Help Us
- Flame of Beauty, Culture, Love, Joy
- The Flame of the Heart
- From My Heart — Volume I (Poetry)
- Hiawatha and the Great Peace
- The Hidden Glory of the Inner Man
- I Was
- Joy and Healing
- Leadership Vol. I
- Leadership Vol. II
- Leadership Vol. III
- Leadership Vol. IV
- Leadership Vol. V
- Legend of Shamballa
- The Mystery of Self-Image
- The Mysteries of Willpower
- New Dimensions in Healing
- Olympus World Report... The Year 3000
- One Hundred Names of God
- Other Worlds
- The Psyche and Psychism
- The Psychology of Cooperation and Group Consciousness
- The Purpose of Life
- The Science of Becoming Oneself
- The Science of Meditation
- The Sense of Responsibility in Society
- Sex, Family, and the Woman in Society
- The Solar Angel
- Spiritual Regeneration
- Spring of Prosperity
- The Subconscious Mind and the Chalice
- Symphony of the Zodiac
- Talks on Agni
- Thought & the Glory of Thinking
- Triangles of Fire
- Unusual Court
- Woman, Torch of the Future
- The Year 2000 & After

Booklets

- The Art of Visualization — Simply Presented
- The Chalice in Agni Yoga Literature
- Cornerstones of Health
- A Daily Discipline of Worship
- Discipleship in Action
- Duties of Grandparents

- Earrings for Business People
- Earthquakes and Disasters — What the Ageless Wisdom Tells Us
- Fiery Carriage and Drugs
- Five Great Mantrams of the New Age
- Hierarchy and the Plan
- How to Find Your Level of Meditation
- Inner Blooming
- Irritation — The Destructive Fire
- Mental Exercises
- Nachiketas
- New Beginnings
- Practical Spirituality
- Questioning Traveler and Karma
- Saint Sergius
- Synthesis

Booklets (Excerpts and Compilations)

- Angels and Devas
- Building Family Unity
- Courage
- Daily Spiritual Striving
- First Steps Toward Freedom
- Prayers, Mantrams, and Invocations
- The Psychology of Cooperation
- Responsibility
- Responsibility and Business
- Responsibilities of Fathers
- Responsibilities of Mothers Success
- Torchbearers
- What to Look for in the Heart of Your Partner

Videos

- The Seven Rays Interpreted
- Why Drugs Are Dangerous
- Lecture Videos by Author (list available)

Music

- A Touch of Heart (CD only)
- Dance of the Zodiac
- Far Horizons
- Fire Blossom
- Go In Beauty (songs by Torkom Saraydarian sung by choir)
- Infinity
- Lao Tse
- Light Years Ahead
- Lily in Tibet
- Misty Mountain
- Piano Composition
- Rainbow
- Spirit of My Heart
- Sun Rhythms
- Tears of My Joy
- Toward Freedom
- 1994 Annual Convention Special Edition — Synthesizer Music

For complete catalog of Books, Booklets, Music, Audio and Video tapes by Torkom Saraydarian contact:

T.S.G. Publishing Foundation, Inc.
P.O. Box 7068
Cave Creek, AZ 85327–7068 United States of America

TEL: (602) 502–1909
FAX: (602) 502–0713

E-Mail:
webmaster@tsg-publishing.com

Visit our web-site at:
www.tsg-publishing.com

About the Publisher

T.S.G. Publishing Foundation, Inc. is a non-profit, tax exempt organization. Founded on November 30, 1987 in Los Angeles, California, it relocated to Cave Creek, Arizona on January 1, 1994.

Our purpose is to be a pathway for self-transformation. We are fully devoted to publishing, teaching, and distributing the creative works of Torkom Saraydarian.

Our bookstore in Cave Creek and our online bookstore at our web site *www.tsg-publishing.com* offer the complete collection of the creative works for sale and distribution. Our newsletter OUTREACH contains thought provoking articles excerpted from these books. We also conduct weekly classes, special training seminars, and home study meditation courses.

Please contact us or visit our web site *www.tsg-publishing.com* if you wish to have additional information about our organization and our activities.

Ordering Information

Write to us for additional information regarding:
— Free catalog of author's books and music tapes
— Complete list of lecture tapes and videos ($2 postage for each list)
— Placement on mailing list for continuous updates
— A free copy of our newsletter *Outreach* and schedule of events
— Book Club (Receive a 20% discount with each new release by Torkom Saraydarian. Each new book is mailed to you automatically as soon as it is released.)

Additional copies of ***Woman, Torch of the Future***
U.S. $18.00

Postage within U.S.A. — $5.00 plus applicable state sales tax
International postage: Contact us for surface or air rates.

T.S.G. Publishing Foundation, Inc.
P.O. Box 7068
Cave Creek, AZ 85327–7068
United States of America
TEL: (480) 502–1909
FAX: (480) 502–0713
E-Mail: webmaster@tsg-publishing.com
Web-site: www.tsg-publishing.com

Participate in the Vision for the Future

Contribute to the Torkom Saraydarian Book Fund

My Pledge:

☐ One-time: $ _____ ☐ Annually: $ _____ ☐ Monthly: $ _____

Name: _____

Address: _____

City: _____

State: _____ Zip: _____

Country: _____

Tel #: (_____) _____ – _____

E-mail address: _____

Method of Payment:

☐ Check/U.S. Money Order   ☐ Visa   ☐ MasterCard

Account #: _____ – _____ – _____ – _____

Exp. date: _____ / _____

Please send to:

T.S.G. Publishing Foundation, Inc. ✧ Attn: Book Fund
P.O. Box 7068 ✧ Cave Creek, AZ 85327 ✧ U.S.A.

Tel: (480) 502-1909 ✧ Fax: (480) 502-0713

E-Mail: webmaster@tsg-publishing.com
Web-site: www.tsg-publishing.com

T.S.G. Publishing Foundation, Inc. is a tax-exempt, non-profit organization.